THEATRE SY M
A PUBLICATION OF THE SOUTHEAS CE

Outdoor Perf

Volume 17

Published by the

Southeastern Theatre Conference and

The University of Alabama Press

THEATRE SYMPOSIUM is published annually by the Southeastern Theatre Conference, Inc. (SETC), and by The University of Alabama Press. SETC nonstudent members receive the journal as a part of their membership under rules determined by SETC. For information on membership write to SETC, P.O. Box 9868, Greensboro, NC 27429-0868. All other inquiries regarding subscriptions, circulation, purchase of individual copies, and requests to reprint materials should be addressed to The University of Alabama Press, Box 870380, Tuscaloosa, AL 35487-0380.

THEATRE SYMPOSIUM publishes works of scholarship resulting from a single-topic meeting held on a southeastern university campus each spring. A call for papers to be presented at that meeting is widely publicized each autumn for the following spring. Information about the next symposium is available from the editor, J. K. Curry, Department of Theatre and Dance, P.O. Box 7364, Wake Forest University, Winston-Salem, NC, 27109, curryjk@wfu.edu.

THEATRE SYMPOSIUM
A PUBLICATION OF THE SOUTHEASTERN THEATRE CONFERENCE

Volume 17

Contents

2009

Introduction

The topic of outdoor drama seemed quite attractive for the second of two symposia under my editorship. My scholarly interest is focused mainly on comedy, but that particular subject furnished the theme for the 2007 Theatre Symposium event at West Virginia University in Morgantown, where I teach (please see *Theatre Symposium* 16). The topic for the second event and its location took me out of my comfort zone into an intellectual and geographical area that would not only furnish material for this volume but would collaterally add to my own understanding of the range and variety of what constitutes outdoor drama.

The location of any symposium event ideally reflects on the topic in some way, grounding the subject in a context that augments both the ideas of the symposium and the experiences of the participants. Once the *Theatre Symposium* Steering Committee of the Southeastern Theatre Conference, specifically Phil G. Hill of Furman University, described the Institute of Outdoor Drama (IOD) at the University of North Carolina, I knew that Chapel Hill had to be the location of the seventeenth Theatre Symposium event.

Moreover, important people associated with the outdoor historical drama still lived in or near Chapel Hill: Mark R. Sumner, a writer of outdoor drama and a former director of the IOD; Rob Franklin Fox, its current director; and Scott J. Parker, Fox's predecessor at the IOD, a former editor of *Theatre Symposium*, and a former president of the Southeastern Theatre Conference. The best-case scenario, therefore, was to find a way to involve all three of these men whose careers spoke directly to the topic at hand. Happily, the three of them graciously and eagerly lent their time and expertise as the keynote speakers of the event. Chapel Hill promised to be a fabulous setting for the event.

The call for papers invited presentations on all manner of outdoor drama, from ancient Greek theatre, which by necessity took place outdoors, to the plays that are still performed today in many parts of the world. Panels convened on historical productions, such seemingly esoteric topics as popular celebrations after the French Revolution and micro-performances in contemporary society. Organizing the panels fulfilled the promise of the call for papers: the event examined outdoor drama in new and exciting ways.

The panels, however, challenged the notion that the event concerned outdoor *historical* drama of the kind with which the keynote speakers usually dealt. Instead, given the varied topics of papers presented, and the interests of some current scholarship in the theatre (e.g., performance studies), the title of *Theatre Symposium* 17 more appropriately morphed from "Outdoor Drama" to "Outdoor Performance."

The event, and the essays in this volume that emerged from it, combined not only a keynote roundtable that dealt with the outdoor historical drama from the point of view of writing and production concerns but also essays that investigated performance in some of those well-known titles or in venues that stretched the definition of "Outdoor Historical Drama." And so, the title of the symposium changed its perceived emphasis from that term to the broader "Outdoor Performance."

The present volume consists of the extended keynote roundtable, six articles that reflect the range of panels and topics at the event, and the give-and-take that generated the Symposium Response that synthesized some of the intersections between the traditional and the newest performances outdoors—performances that extend the boundaries and call into question the definition of "theatre space."

Holding the Theatre Symposium event in North Carolina, the home of many of the greatest examples of the outdoor historical drama, provided several benefits beyond the IOD and the informative papers. The University of North Carolina campus at Chapel Hill houses a professional regional theatre, PlayMakers Repertory Company, and many attendees of the symposium enjoyed a performance of Peter Shaffer's *Amadeus* (alas, indoors!) on Saturday night. The Friday-night plans supplied an interesting problem of how to provide a convivial scene at dinner for the members of this year's event to mix and share their ideas. Again, the IOD staff assisted in the planning by suggesting a dinner at a restaurant associated with an actual outdoor theatre, the Snow Camp Theatre in rural Snow Camp, North Carolina. The attendees even benefited from an impromptu, albeit off-season, tour of the working outdoor theatre. Thus, a few minutes' drive out of town provided both a delicious meal and an experience intimately tied to the topic of the event.

On Saturday afternoon the event witnessed an unplanned combination of the traditional and the most avant-garde when, during a tour of the Forrest Theatre on the UNC campus by Scott Parker, a posse of black-clad parkour performers swept through the theatre around us—immediately after the last paper of the morning session had described the newest "rage" in outdoor performance, parkour. Everyone appreciated the instant karma demonstrated in the spectacle. Then, to put the finishing touches on the experience of *real* outdoor drama, the skies opened up and forced Parker into a "rain tempo" to finish his remarks at the outdoor venue.

Later in the afternoon, Rob Fox provided participants with a tour of the nearby Institute of Outdoor Drama; the institute contains memorabilia and historical archives that encapsulate the history of outdoor historical dramas, pageants, and Shakespeare festivals in this country and elsewhere. The participants, who all had an invested interest in the topic, leafed through materials that Fox had drawn from the collection for our edification.

The essays contained herein begin with a fascinating report: "'No Roof Except the Sky': The Rise and Fall of Airdomes in American Popular Entertainment," by Landis K. Magnuson, takes readers on a tour of performance spaces that came to be called "airdomes," which provided open-air shows primarily in the Midwest in the first half of the last century. Next, Jane Barnette's "Rail-izing the Nation along Lake Michigan: The *Wheels a-Rolling* Pageant" further examines outdoor performance of a kind that stretches traditional definitions to include celebratory pageants.

Conference presentations sometimes dealt with very site-specific productions, as the next entries in this volume demonstrate: "Mormon Pageants as American Historical Performance" reflects Martha S. LoMonaco's research into a civic and religious pageant-drama performed not in Utah but in Nauvoo, Illinois. A pair of participants from another outdoor drama, Charlotte Headrick and Andrew Vorder Bruegge, recount their experiences in "'Look at the Moon': Hunter Hills Theatre; Outdoor Drama in the Smokies." The presentation of their firsthand experience from the participants' point of view further argues for the more inclusive volume title of "Outdoor Performance." Angela Sweigart-Gallagher continues the exploration of traditional outdoor historical drama in "The Promise of Democracy: Imagining National Community in Paul Green's *The Lost Colony*." Sweigart-Gallagher offers insights into the ramifications of the Federal Theatre Project supporting the growing outdoor performance venues and so rounds out our discussion of such productions.

Finally, as mentioned above, the volume contains a discussion of a phenomenon that breaks with almost every expectation that the phrase "outdoor performance" provides. Jeanmarie Higgins's "The Revitalization of Space: Freestyle Parkour and Its Audiences" describes an ever-changing performance space and the practitioners who make use of existing architecture. The level of site specificity may exist only in the minds of the performers, and few anticipated that the spaces themselves, such as the Forrest Theatre, would host such performances.

The Symposium Response concluded the event and concludes *Theatre Symposium* 17. The session gave the keynote speakers and attendees the opportunity to respond to scholarship and research that supported their experiences or challenged their conception of how outdoor performance exists today—as drama or in some other mode. I count myself among those whose experience and understanding of the topic expanded mightily in the short weekend of the event, and I invite readers to enjoy what this edition of *Theatre Symposium* offers on the subject. As I look at the whole of the volume, I realize it contains thoughts and experiences from at least three generations of outdoor drama scholars, practitioners, and enthusiasts.

I have been looking forward especially to thanking the many people who have helped to make this all possible—all that I have described above, and the many other papers that were presented at the event and that may have entered this volume as a comment or consideration in one of the discussions. As always with *Theatre Symposium,* the contents of the printed journal and the experience of the SETC annual event relate but do not exactly overlap. My thanks therefore begin with all of the event's participants.

Further, the authors of the essays contained here, participants themselves, deserve even more thanks for their fastidious attention to shaping their conference papers into more lengthy and formal scholarship.

The participants who brought such vast experience to the event and whose insights absolutely made the weekend possible, Mark R. Sumner, Scott J. Parker, and Rob Franklin Fox, certainly receive my most heartfelt and undying thanks.

The logistics of the event came together as the result of many helpful and generous people. The staff at the IOD, especially Susan Phillips, helped determine food plans, among other decisions. The UNC Department of Dramatic Art, especially John Rogers Harris and Herb Garman, made it possible for us to use space in the Dramatic Art building for the Saturday panels.

Our editorial board, again this year, provided necessary suggestions for improvement of the journal essays; no journal could exist without the help of such colleagues. My especial thanks to Scott Phillips of Auburn University, my immediate predecessor, who again read submissions and provided guidance, and to the associate editor for my two editions of the Theatre Symposium, J. K. Curry of Wake Forest University; best wishes to her, also, for her tenure as the next volume's editor.

The *Theatre Symposium* Steering Committee (especially Phil G. Hill), the Publications Committee, and everyone at the home office of the Southeastern Theatre Conference, led by Betsey Baun, deserve and receive my gratitude as well.

My colleagues and the office staff at The College of Creative Arts, and the Division of Theatre and Dance, of West Virginia University deserve thanks for their help with my attendance at the event and the incidental costs and demands of editing this manuscript. Speaking of the manuscript: finally, to Dan Waterman at The University of Alabama Press I offer my thanks for the advice and instruction for the development and finalization of the manuscript. I offer thanks also to the staff and others whose hard work shepherds this project through the publication process.

JAY MALARCHER
WEST VIRGINIA UNIVERSITY

Theatre Symposium

Keynote Roundtable

Saturday, April 12, 2008

Rob Franklin Fox, Scott J. Parker, and
Mark R. Sumner; Jay Malarcher, moderator

JAY MALARCHER [JM]: Okay, good afternoon, again, everyone. This is the centerpiece of the conference in my mind, the roundtable discussion by those we have in our midst, the resident experts of the historical drama and the outdoor drama represented here. Mr. Mark Sumner, Mr. Scott Parker, and Mr. Rob Fox are the brain trust that we're going to listen to today. I asked them not to—it wasn't necessary for them to prepare a formal paper, so don't be expecting that. I asked them each to come up with something to say based on their interests, their background, what they have derived from the study or the historical inquest of drama outdoors. I'm just going to leave it to them. They can do a free-for-all, and when they've decided they've had enough, we can open it up to questions and force more out of them . . . so this is really a treat for us. And so, here's our roundtable.

SCOTT J. PARKER [SJP]: We've had enough.

JM: That's cheating!

SJP: Rob has allowed me to go first. Mark, I guess, have y'all met Mark? Mark was the second director of the Institute of Outdoor Drama [IOD]. The Institute opened up in 1963. Bill Trotman was the first director, and he lasted one year before he ran screaming into the night, and Mark was gracious enough to leave academia, well, and to come into academia. But he was teaching up at Mary Washington in Fredericksburg, Virginia. Did I get that right?

MARK R. SUMNER [MRS]: That's right.

SJP: And came in 1964 and ran the Institute for twenty-five years, and really made it what it is today. I think of Mark as the Grand Poobah of outdoor historical drama in this country. He—to mix a metaphor—he was also a bit of Johnny Appleseed. He went around the country planting outdoor dramas all over the place. So he's our resident historian. And then, Mark went fishing in 1989, and I was lucky enough to follow in his footsteps. I was down at *The Lost Colony*, and I came in 1990. Then, I went fishing seven months ago. Rob, after a national search, they found Rob right here at our own backdoor! Rob was the general manager here at PlayMakers Repertory Company. They went through a whole search, and they ended up right here with Rob, so we're very lucky to have him. Rob's been on board now for seven or eight months. We really haven't collaborated very much about what we're going to say today, and I've got a wonderful story to illustrate. Some of you may know this story—it's a theatre legend. It has to do with the Barrymore family, our royal family of theatre. John and Ethel and Lionel and now Drew . . . Who were the other Barrymores? There must have been some others. Anyhow, this is a story about John and Ethel. The story goes that every now and again they would do a show together. They'd mostly do classics. They were doing a show in New York, a Shakespeare play the name of which I don't remember anymore. They had a reputation—the whole family has a reputation of getting into alcohol a bit. But they had a policy between the two of them that one of them would drink one night, and the other one would drink the next night. They never both drank on the same night when they were doing a show. But they got confused one night, and both of them came in a little tipsy, and they were well into the show and they both went up. I mean, both went up at the same time, and some little girl offstage left is the prompter and she's going like this [frantically goes through papers], "Jesus! Where is it?!" And she finds it, and she feeds them the line. Ethel is reported to have said, "We *know* what the line is, damnit! We just don't know who says it!" Well, we know what we're supposed to say to you today, but I'm not quite sure who's going to say what!

We do know Mark, as I say, is our historian, and we thought it might be a good idea if he would set this up by giving you some history of the outdoor historical drama movement. We don't know nothin' about your parkour and angels and all that other kind of stuff . . . looking through glasses and mirrors [a reference to previous presentations during the day]. We know about outdoor historical drama, and that's what we're going to talk about today. So Mark, you want to start us off?

MRS: Well, I don't know. Perhaps this big sales pitch he gave on me is going to cost me in a little bit, but I want to set you straight: I'm not really an expert at anything. I thought I was at one point.

Al Bell designed the amphitheatre down for *The Lost Colony* at the coast. It was built by the WPA, and that whole project was a Federal Theatre Project in the middle-to-late '30s. I went with Al Bell's son, Richard, who was at that point then a full-fledged landscape architect and knew his amphitheatres because his father had built the first big one on the East Coast. So we were to go with Paul Green to a place in Maryland that shall be nameless. We were going at the urging of Paul, who had been approached about writing an outdoor historical drama for this community. Now I've been involved [at] several places before—now this particular occasion his wife, Elizabeth, was with him—and they got there just a little earlier and had met most of the local people that were involved in this little community, which was kind of "on the road" if you went from Washington, DC, out to the beaches. And there are a number of beaches starting in Delaware and going all the way down to the Atlantic tip of Maryland. It was really sort of interesting: Richard, who was going to look for amphitheatre sites; and me, who was going to try to talk to them about how outdoor dramas were put together and how they were done and make them acquainted with the fact that they cost a lot of money. Because everybody in casts that were over one hundred people—everybody got paid—means you really have to get people to come into the theatre. So I thought maybe I had a wee bit of expertise on that. I had been—not teaching—but managing a show in Kentucky, producing, called *Home Is the Hunter,* an outdoor historic drama, before I came back down to Chapel Hill and got involved.

In any case, we arrived at the town. Richard was coming separately from me, so when I drove in, I came to a very quiet little town square. I didn't see much town around it, not many residences; there were not many stores of any kind. I looked, but the highway went straight through on the way to the beach. I thought, "Well, I don't know, maybe I'm just looking in the wrong part." In a little bit, Richard arrived, and we went to the town hall to meet the committee that wanted to find out how to produce and where in their area that they could produce an outdoor historical drama. I said when we first met, I asked the man who was in charge. I said, "What is the story that you want to tell?" "Oh, oh," he said, "We'll talk about that later." So we went on, and they took us—it was the first or second of December, and it started to spit snow. We were walking around where these fellas had found areas where the state was going to buy land for them and put a park, and where they could put an amphitheatre.

Actually, we did find several places where they might do that if they could talk the state into it. In the meantime, of course, the snow got a little worse, and it got a little worse. And, as time went on, it got a little worse. It began to be visible all over everything. The spitting snow was getting a little heavier, and all we were getting was great enthusiasm from a bunch of citizens—most of whom had nothing to do with the entertainment business—but to do with some other kind of business, who could just *visualize* the amphitheatre on the side of the slope, looking down to the stage, and in the amphitheatre were people sitting in seats. It's very hard when people get that in their heads to remind them that you have to do something about it. So that became our job. I went back as Dick had finally said, "Well, we've got two or three places that we can suggest that they talk to the state about getting the land." I kept, every once and a while, asking somebody, "What's the story?" Finally, we got back to the country club building, not a huge one but a very nice bar. We're sitting at tables like this [gestures at speakers table], but set in a "T," with people in the committee out there, and head people of the committee here at the table, and Richard Bell was sitting there, and I was sitting up here. I was looking down at him when finally they asked me to say something. I said, "Will somebody explain to me exactly what the story is that you want to interest people? What are they coming here to watch?" And there was a silence. A lady sitting down at the side down there said, "Well . . . chicken farming in the eastern United States started *right here* on this site!" Dick Bell's neck got red, starting here [gestures at collar], and the red went right on up. It's hard to explain, but I will just simply say that after that meeting, no further effort was made to produce an outdoor drama in that community.

Well, I'm glad you chuckled at that story. I thought it was pretty good! Proving that I'm an expert, I went down to a place in Texas, on Galveston Island, well, actually the City of Galveston wanted an outdoor historical drama. They had already had Paul there. There was much talk going on with the state at that point because they wanted to put it on state property. We had a good talk, and it was perfectly clear that they had the political strength. They had some theatre artists, some college people. They had a huge banking foundation—not just two banks—but a foundation that two banks supported. We felt, as we talked, very good about the whole thing. Finally, I told them this story. Finally, when I came to the part where the lady said, "Chicken farming in the eastern United States started right here in this county," people laughed so hard one fella fell out of his seat, the ladies were banging on the table, everybody thought it was a good story—but not for chuckles! Unfortunately, they said, "Oh, well just forty miles up the road is the biggest house of prostitution in Texas called the Chicken Ranch!" I said, "It'll never make a play." So you know what kind of expert I am.

I was lucky enough, and I have to talk about myself just a little to go back and string some of the past together to talk about the outdoor that started drama. I love outdoor Shakespeare. I have done, on many occasions, everything I could to help an outdoor Shakespeare—even to be in one, although I'm not sure that was a lot of help. My love is what I found here. Now, I mentioned yesterday to some of the folks who were there, that my first job in theatre, when I was very young, was to help a group, or worked for a group, called Herrington-Russell Festivals that did field pageants. We talked, or at least I tried to explain a little yesterday about what a "field pageant" is, and there are companies that still do that for communities. It is a very reasonable way to get a big colorful show on to help the county fair, or to help the county historically, or whatever. I'm not knocking it—they paid my way for a while. They also got me introduced down here in Chapel Hill to the staff of the Carolina Playmakers. I happened, in high school, to write a play that happened to win a statewide contest, and the folks from Chapel Hill invited the production winners and the playwriting winners to put their plays on here in Chapel Hill in a spring festival. They did that every year. I expect it worked really well for the drama department as a recruiting tool, but it also got a lot of kids who hadn't thought about it wanting to go to college. I really enjoyed being here, and on that occasion, that first trip down when they did a play of mine, people paid me a lot of attention because I'd written a play. I thought it was great that I'd written that many pages and nobody had thrown them away! But, apparently, the little play did pretty well, and it was about Indians, and that was sort of colorful, and I was very lucky. A lot of people then expected me to write another one, which I did later, which is not the story.

One of the things I did on the first trip down was to meet a man named Paul Green. I didn't know anything about *The Lost Colony* until I met him, and someone explained that he'd written a huge outdoor play that was being done down in Manteo, North Carolina. Well I knew Herrington-Russell Festivals had done a pageant there in 1935, and this was a couple of years—four years after that that I met Mr. Green. So I connected the two as well. The people in Manteo hadn't liked my company, but they'd liked Mr. Green, and I found out that the university here in Chapel Hill put its staff to making *The Lost Colony* work. Also, the Federal Theater Project assisted it. The lead actors in that play its first year were equity members from New York. Carefully selected, not only for their abilities as performers but their abilities to adapt to the changing situation of moving down to Manteo, which at that time was a little fishing village and didn't have much except the state site that represented the place where the original lost colony had been on Roanoke Island. So with that in mind, and with an interest in coming back here (which I eventually did after World War II), just getting that nibble about what outdoor drama was about, as it turned out, was very important to me. I was already used to looking up at the sky like that in the afternoon, wondering if we were going to play that night, because I'd been doing that with the pageant company from time to time. By the way, you can always tell if somebody has had a bit of a turn in outdoor drama because they all have problems with the neck, right here [gestures to neck]. Is it going to rain? Is it not going to rain? Are we going to play? Are we not going to play? And at what tempo? Well, you hear lots of jokes about rain tempo, but it's true in many companies.

In any case, I did have the occasion early on, by coming to this university as part of their state festival in both high school and in college. But I did get a chance to ask Paul Green what the outdoor history play was that everybody was talking about because they said it was different. It used a lot of music and dance. He said, "Music has great power. Dance, the body in motion, has great power, and when I add that to the dialogue, and the costuming, and the other arts, I have done something that people will forever remember."

Maybe I can follow up: Many years later, he made another comment that carries that a step further, but, as I was listening, he said, "I handle it like I would being an orchestra conductor. I use the music and bring it in at certain times, and at other times I turn the storytelling into dance. I use them to tell the story . . . not just for themselves. Not just because the song is nice, but because the song helps disclose the characters and tell the story." He said, "I feel cramped on the indoor stages. I can do anything the technicians can manage outdoors, but I can't do that indoors." He really was interested in this and developed, after several attempts on Broadway, to spread out the performance technique. There's a play called *Johnny Johnson*, by Paul Green. If you read it, you will find *The Lost Colony* and other plays forecast in it. He's an interesting writer. He was a farmer and farm kid when he grew up, and his association with the earth and its source of life worked into everything he wrote, I think. So he had very strong goals of things he wanted to disclose to people that drove him into this form of expression. I remember, one of his plays, he says, "The horse falls down dead, but turns and grins at the driver." Now how do you stage that on an indoor stage? But he actually wrote that in a play.

Anyway, Paul was sort of the source of pressing for a new way to handle outdoor things. Pageants didn't interest him. Pageants interested the man who started the Playmaker program here, Fred[erick H.] Koch. As a matter of fact, when he was in North Dakota, Fred did some pageants there and was well known for them, when they brought him down here. Even before *The Lost Colony* he helped produce a thing in Raleigh called *Raleigh, Shepherd of the Ocean*. That was a big field pageant. So there were people pushing the limits all the time at the staff of this university. Sam Selden, who was the first director of *The Lost Colony,* was a staff member here and a close assistant to Professor Koch. Selden had been raised in China, where his parents were missionaries, and came on with a number of approaches in staging that play that we're doing differently. One of the things they found in writing these plays, of course, is that the acting has to be different. You aren't involved in pulling the audience up on the stage. What you are doing with your actors and your directing is creating the focus and pushing the play out to them, which is one of the reasons why side stages were adapted for the outdoor drama so that they can play plays almost continuously like a movie because you turn lights on here, you turn them on here, you turn them on here, and you turn them on in another side stage depending on how you want to move the action and the scene changes. It gave a great deal of flexibility to what was being done. So we had to alter the acting a little bit. Anybody who's going to perform in these plays needed to be able to speak to fifteen hundred, eighteen hundred seats. Some of them were a little bigger than that. The microphones that they had in those days were not very good, and they would record any blast of wind, even your breath if you were close to it, with a roar on the microphone. We've got much better equipment today at many of the outdoor dramas, of course, and musically, but this fella's gonna talk something about that.

My interest after I got back here was pretty great because my boss was called upon to go down to *The Lost Colony* as the manager, and I ended up helping him with numbers of things on the business staff while I was a grad student working in the business office here with the Playmakers. I sort of became acquainted with a lot of the early people of *The Lost Colony,* as well as some of the things they had to change in their techniques, and it left me with a great interest. I went on and did other things in the theatre. I quit writing, mainly because I wanted to direct, and I did several years, and acted. So I sort of went this way, and outdoor drama was getting more and more complex, happening in more and more places, and more and more people from here were going to other colleges and universities and training other people who had the speech patterns and who had an awareness that you couldn't just act with your face in outdoor drama. You had to act with your body, and hand gestures, and the stance. All of it becomes very important in projecting things out to the audience . . . but it's still acting. It's just an extension that used to be fairly typical in big indoor theatres, but gradually shifted away as the movies came in and as the theatres got smaller and dropped below a thousand seats in many places. Obviously, if you're going to do these plays and have big casts and do big technical things, you've gotta have a lot of money. How they put these things together in those days . . . [gestures to other speakers] they're going to talk about how you do it today. I'm out of that. I don't raise money anymore. The way people did that, and it worked, was to develop a nonprofit corporation. They got all the interested people in the community who'd be interested in telling their story . . . whatever it was. Whether it was about a historical place that they had there that people could come see, that was important to the region or the nation, or whether it was people who were born and raised there, or whether it was an action that occurred there like a battle or a big legislative decision—whatever it was that occurred there that affected the region and perhaps the nation. If you didn't have this connection, it was very difficult to build the interest necessary to bring a thousand, twelve hundred, fifteen hundred, people in a night who don't live there because when you start these dramas, of course, you're repeating to the people in the county and whoever else you can reach. But as a few seasons go on, they've all seen the show. They may come back after a few years. They may bring visitors, and you try to encourage that as they bring family members or business visitors to come and see the summer show, but the play has to stand as an impact that will be carried home by the audience. We did a—speaking of the expert business—we were doing a survey when I arrived here on why people attended outdoor drama. Where did they first hear of it? What attracted them? We had gotten a lot of information back, and it disclosed that most people said that they'd heard about it by word of mouth. And maybe next, at that time, it was television, and radio, and newspapers. Newspapers were very popular and kept around when they had the ad in it so people could refer back to it, but the first awareness often came from the television or radio. We had this worked out. The only thing we found was that the word of mouth, which was so great, did not occur unless the media work had been there in advance. If there was no media work, there wasn't any word of mouth. Even though people were seeing it and going home and talking favorably, it was that double-reinforcement of the media and the word of mouth on how good you were to get people to come. Well, this report had been written and was in the office when I had gone somewhere out of town, and the promotion director from *Unto These Hills* in the western part of North Carolina came by the office to get information on attendance, that is the numbers, because they always put out of their department a story about how they were the biggest show in the country. They had bigger attendance, more attendance, than anyone else, and that was what she was working on. However, she happened to see this, down there, and looked at it, and asked my secretary if she could have a copy of it. My secretary told her we hadn't released that yet, but I think it's all right if you take it to look at it. Well, I got back here, and in a day or two I had mail come in, envelopes come into the office from a number of newspapers. People I knew. Unfortunately, what they had in the envelopes were copy of the story with notes on them.

The story started: "It is not advertising in newspapers, radio, and television which brings people into the outdoor dramas. It is that mysterious thing called word of mouth." I'll never forget that sentence. The fellow who ran the news bureau here at the time, Pete, Pete knew that I had worked for the newspapers and the radio stations and that I probably would turn him out a good story. He never read it. So, the story went out to the state without anybody reviewing it first. Well, you don't really want to twist the tail of the people who are kind to you and who give you lots of free stuff. So I got a lot of comments. Most of them were like, "Here! Here! Do you really mean this?" Or things like that because the sense of humor at that time amongst the newspaper people was pretty good, but it was very embarrassing to the news bureau and very embarrassing to me to have kicked them in the shins when this came out.

And so, you just have to remember, when we speak of experts, you have to qualify it every time. So that was not an "expert" action on my part or my office's part. Now, I have sort of given, I hope, a background for this and for some of the people. I think that most of the faculty and staff of the Carolina Playmakers came to a point, I was long gone and doing something else at the time, they came to the point where they might go out and direct the outdoor drama, but it was very hard for those who had the time and interest and wanted to go. It was very hard for them to cover all that was happening with the Carolina Playmakers. It was getting tougher and tougher for them to be gone and direct an outdoor drama instead of cover the work here anyway. What happened was . . . with the help of then North Carolina governor Terry Sanford, and with pressure always from Paul Green—but also from some of the political leaders—the university was asked to set up an agency to help the UNC Department of Dramatic Art serve the people all over the country who were writing the university to find out, "How do you put together a two-million-dollar outdoor drama? What do you have to put in the theatre? How do you go about it? Who do you talk to? If we've talked to people about it, whose work we liked, can you help them to get on the right track?" And that's what the institute was set up to do: to research and find out, and to do things like we're doing today—talk to people and answer questions, which you're going to get a chance to do.

They made a couple of tries and couldn't cover the budget, so the attempts at the institute were sort of experimental. Finally, in 1964, through Terry Sanford's efforts, and Johnny Lee, and a few other people like that, the university got the money to set it up. It's been continued now since 1964 as a public service agency on top of being a receipt-supported research agency. Research that's done and the records are kept and things you can find out, if you want to do this kind of thing big-time. The Institute of Outdoor Drama, set up by the University of North Carolina at Chapel Hill, to help the public all over the country. And thanks for this.

SJP: I told y'all, all we had to do was wind him up and punch the button, and here he goes. Rob, you want to go next?

Rob Franklin Fox [RFF]: I will go next. I'm going to read my comments, although it is quite new for me. It will—you will very quickly realize that my background is in general management, and I came up through the box office, and that's probably going to be very apparent from some of the remarks that I have to make. *(Reading)* "There are those who say *The Lost Colony* is dead. They will claim that theatrical production cannot be expected to survive a run for more than twenty years in the same location, with the same script." It says, "They cite the difficulties of other productions to show that the field is overcrowded. And use this as the basis for their prediction that *The Lost Colony* must soon fold up. I'm not one of these. There are still others of these who say that the solution to *The Lost Colony*'s problem is to move the show somewhere else or replace the present show with another one. I'm not one of these. There are still others who say *The Lost Colony* needs new management, that with new management all the troubles will be solved. I'm not one of these."

What I've just read is the opening of a speech given by a board member, David Stick, at an annual meeting of the Roanoke Island Historical Association, the producing organization of *The Lost Colony*. The date of the speech was December 1, 1959. The spring 2008 edition of *Southern Theatre*—the cover story was entitled "Outdoor Drama Weathers Storm." The truth is . . . the audience attendance to outdoor drama has downsized during recent years. The truth is, we have to find new ways to compete. Does this mean a new play? Does this mean we need new management? Does this mean that we need new locations? I don't have the solutions, but I do believe that we need to be asking new questions. Not the same old questions that we've been asking for fifty years. Some of the most important research that the institute conducts each year is the annual survey of outdoor dramas throughout the country.

The institute primarily works with three categories of theatres. We have them divided into outdoor historical dramas, such as *The Sword of Peace* in Snow Camp, North Carolina, where we visited last night, or Paul Green's *The Lost Colony;* outdoor religious dramas; and outdoor Shakespeare festivals. The total attendance for the Institute of Outdoor Drama theatres, the IOD theatres, was 1,811,000 for 2007. That was essentially a 0 percent change from the year before. Although that number is technically smaller than the number from the 2006 total attendance of 1,900,000 roughly . . . they were close enough. The deficit has to do with fewer theatres reporting true attendance numbers. Ninety-seven reported in 2006, and eighty-three reported in 2007. Now, let me say that fewer theatres reporting does not mean theatres closing. Yes, we did have three closings, but there were also others that did not produce productions that fit into the three categories that I mentioned earlier. The bulk of the drop had to do with administrative turnover and some staff downsizing where the information was lost or never kept track of in the first place.

However, when you compare just the theatres that participated in the 2006 survey and the 2007, the difference is fewer than five hundred. That raw number does not take into account rainouts of the varying schedules. The trend is basically flat for all production groups. Total attendance of each group was within 2 percent last year. Twelve of twenty-four history plays, 50 percent, showed improved attendance over last year. Total attendance for the history group last year was around four hundred thousand. Four of the eight religious dramas, again, 50 percent, showed an improved attendance over last year. Total attendance for the religious dramas was around 268,000. Twenty-four of the forty-eight Shakespeare productions, 50 percent, showed improved attendance over last year. Total Shakespeare attendance was 1,140,000. However, it is worth pointing out that that category does include both pay productions and free productions. Since 2004, attendance to all outdoor drama has essentially been flat. This is not just true for last year, but we have now seen three straight years with 0 percent change. To give an example, *Tecumseh!* in Chillicothe, Ohio, increased by 1 percent in total attendance for the last year with a total attendance of forty-eight thousand. That's roughly forty-six thousand paid and two thousand comped. They had an average paying nightly attendance of 666 this past summer. That was actually an increase over the previous year.

I mention *Tecumseh!* because in the *Southern Theatre* article, when asked about the health of outdoor historical drama, *Tecumseh!* producer Marion Waggoner said, "Perhaps I'm a dinosaur, but I don't see the big comet in the sky." That sentiment was echoed at this past fall's National Conference on Outdoor Drama. Attendees commented on the shift in attitude from previous years. What I'm trying to say is that there was a lot more optimism in the room. If that is the case, then it stands to reason that we have seen gloom in the past. The truth is that from 2001 to 2004, attendance for all outdoor dramas was down 21 percent. History plays went down approximately 22 percent. Shakespeare plays went down approximately 15 percent. I don't have the breakdown, but paid Shakespeares were down a little more. Free Shakespeares weren't quite so much, but a close figure nonetheless.

But what has stunned me the most, I must say, since taking this position in August, is the decline in religious dramas. During the conservative years of the [George W.] Bush administration, we have seen a 36 percent drop in the attendance of religious dramas. That being said, what we know about those who are attending outdoor historical dramas: over 56 percent of the audience has seen the drama before. Of that percentage, only a small group account for the patrons who attend the play regularly or annually. Most of those have not seen the drama in the past five years, and 66 percent have seen other outdoor dramas. I know many who travel around this state attend several of the outdoor dramas in this state. Sixty-two percent live in a two-hundred-mile radius of the theatre. Thirty-eight percent live beyond the two-hundred-mile radius.

Last, I want to mention two other points about ticket-purchasing behavior. One concern that most theatres are having is date of sales. Percentage of patrons who make a last-minute purchase has steadily increased over the last few years, coinciding with some significant drops we've seen in the attendance numbers. Finally, one theatre in particular has—I took this from one particular theatre's survey—when asked, "Would you prefer to buy tickets online?" the answer was 66 percent "Yes." The institute continues to gather data from theatres and theatre patrons regarding demographics and ticket sales. It is our mission to serve as a resource in the field. One of the greatest concerns is the economic downturn and the results that will have on tourism this summer. Outdoor drama is a major training ground for young actors, offering the next generation an opportunity to develop their craft under the stars. I will end by quoting the same speech that I started off with. The conclusion of that speech was "What a wonderful opportunity we have on Roanoke Island."

SJP: Okay. Thank you, sir. Well I thought I would speak to you a little bit about the new outdoor dramas that are in development or that have been in development in my day. It seems forever that I've been out of the loop here . . . for six or seven months. We call these communities that are starting new outdoor dramas—at the institute we refer to them as "Planted Groups." They usually get started because a couple goes off on vacation and they see an outdoor drama. Mom says to Pop, "Look at all these people out here!" and dollar signs start appearing in their eyes, and they say "Whoa! We've got a story we could tell at home!" and they go home and they start talking it up and they get real excited. Then they usually call the management of the outdoor drama they just saw. They say, "Tell us everything you know about outdoor drama in five minutes." That's when they usually hand it off to Rob and to the Institute of Outdoor Drama.

The first question we usually ask these communities is "*Why* do you want to do this?" The two most popular reasons—the reasons that we like to hear the most . . . the number one reason is that they're proud of their heritage . . . of the history of the area. They want to celebrate it, and they want to preserve it. The second most common reason is that they're looking for an economic impact project—some economic development. These, as you can already gather, I'm sure you already know that these outdoor dramas are part of the travel and tourism industry. They've got one foot in the theatre world and one foot in the travel and tourism world, and, incidentally, travel and tourism people don't have a clue about theatre, and I can guarantee you that theatre people don't know anything about travel and tourism. One of the things that the institute does is to speak both languages and to help people understand how this animal works: so economic impact is almost always on their minds. While it's true that some of these outdoor dramas have a significant economic impact—some of the bigger ones that we've been talking about, on a good year, can have an economic impact of twenty or twenty-five million dollars a year—most of these shows are done in small towns, you know, and so that kind of money . . . Boy, you're talking shop, when you start talking that kind of money.

These people who go to the outdoor dramas, and the numbers have changed, as Rob has told you. It used to be, not long ago, before we hit this slump . . . the average distance someone—Mark proved this—

the average distance these families traveled to see an outdoor drama is two hundred miles from home, two hundred miles back home. That's a four-hundred-mile round trip that is squarely in the travel and tourism industry. That's beginning to change some now. Those outdoor dramas that are near major metropolitan areas—for example the Ohio outdoor dramas: *Tecumseh!*, *Blue Jacket*, *Trumpet in the Land* . . . those shows. They've got within a two-hundred-mile radius, they've got twenty-three million people. That's *a lot* of people. *Texas* outdoor drama—Paul Green's show in Amarillo—or, if you're from there, "Amarilla"—they've only got 1.6 million people within two hundred miles. So there's no guarantee that you're going to draw large numbers if you have a lot of people within two hundred miles. Texas outdoor drama had the biggest attendance of all outdoor dramas back in the '70s, '80s, and into the '90s. They'd play to 110,000 people. *The Lost Colony* would be stuck at 80,000 people. They've got maybe 3.5 million people and a lot of fish within a two-hundred-mile radius. So they're clearly part of the travel and tourism industry.

The second question the institute asks when these communities call is—and Mark alluded to this—is "What is the story you want to tell?" Nothing is more important than the story. If you don't have a story to tell that's not a compelling story and will make me want to put the kids in the car and drive two hundred miles, then you've got nothing. You all know the ingredients of a good story. Especially in outdoor drama, conflict is critical. There's a lot of education that goes on, explaining to community leaders what makes a good story. Oftentimes, community leaders don't really know what makes a good story, and I've got a number of stories that I could tell you about that.

It's also important that these smaller communities have tourist infrastructure or services in order to service an increase in tourism. Oftentimes, their appetite is bigger than their stomach. They want to do this large outdoor drama, but they've only got this small mom-and-pop hotel, and that's it. I explain to them that the economic impact is all about "heads in beds" in this business. The money's going to go wherever the tourists spend the night. So we have to go through that explanation. Securing the land is terribly important. It's the biggest stumbling block of starting an outdoor drama by far—getting the land. Mark alluded to the fact that it can be expensive. In my day when we were specking these things out, a major outdoor drama would cost, with the capital campaign, would be in the neighborhood of one-and-a-half to three million dollars, and some of them can go much higher than that.

In my seventeen-and-a-half years at the institute, we did forty-five or fifty of these feasibility studies all over the country. Most of them were small communities. I photocopied a list of them here. We did one in Kodiak, Alaska. Mark helped them start an outdoor drama that ran for twenty-five years. Kodiak, Alaska, is not your major tourist stopover or destination. It ran for twenty-five years, and then they closed it down. They hired the institute to help them get it started again. That was a fun study on Kodiak.

Years ago an outdoor drama started in Tuscumbia, Alabama. Do you know what's in Tuscumbia? That's where Helen Keller lived. And the water pump and all that. They started an outdoor drama down there about Helen Keller—well they did . . . What's the Gibson show? *Miracle Worker*! They did that for years, and then they needed some help keeping it going.

We did a feasibility study for a group in Washington, Georgia. That's another interesting story. This was a . . . very quickly, we're running out of time. This was a Civil War story. They wanted to tell the story about when Jefferson Davis got the hell out of Richmond 'cause all the Yankees were coming. He threw all the gold on a train and headed south. They came to Washington, Georgia, and spent the night. Well, a bunch of local thugs stormed the train and stole the gold—all the Confederate gold. To this day, we don't know where it is. "Good idea," I thought. It didn't go anywhere, but . . . that's another long story.

Hutchinson, Kansas: they called me, and I said, "What happened out there?" They said, "Well, nothing ever happened in Hutchinson, Kansas." Dullest place on the face of the earth, as far as I could tell. "Oh please," they said, "We can taste it! We're going to do an outdoor drama! Oh please come out here!" I said, "I don't hear the story—you've gotta tell me the story!" No story. I finally agreed to go out there, and I took Chris Moe with me, a playwright, who Mark has known for years, to help me find out a story.

Q&A

JM: This seems a good place to begin a discussion, or Q&A session, and I'd like to begin with a question for Mark based on an earlier chat we had about the difference between a pageant and a drama.

MRS: When you speak of pageant, you're talking about a report—in motion and sounds—of events that took place in a particular place, that are important to the people that you expect to come see it. It may have conflict in every one of these sequences. But the sequences are connected by somebody who tells you what the bridge material is, called a narrator. And so we're talking about . . . this happened . . . and then this happened . . . and then this happened, but it might be to different people, it might be ten years apart, it might be important events that are being commemorated in the community and also since they are done loosely without real characterization all kinds of volunteers can play the roles, you don't need actors. It's great if you got some, but you don't have to have them. If you've got a dance school doing part of your work, a couple of church choirs helping in other sequences, and so on. And you rehearse one over here, one over there, maybe even different towns in the county. And your staff just goes around and works with each one on a schedule. You put them all together for a dress rehearsal, which turns young men old and, and the show itself comes off at least partly because it's a mystery.

Audience member's question or comment [Q]: Well, and the word *mystery* there is kind of well chosen because it reminded me of the medieval cycle plays where you have *Noah's Flood* and then *Abraham and Isaac* and so it's basically the continuation of that. As opposed to . . . ?

MRS: Yes and no. No, it's a commemoration which takes that form.

Q: Oh, I see. So it borrows that—

MRS: One does not come from the other. So now if we're talking about a play, we're talking about something [that] has happened to this person or these people. It will be these people by the time your first scene is over. Which causes this to happen, and then that causes that to happen, and its all connected. And then there is a central goal. A central conflict in opposition, of course, may be scattered, but essentially the opposition is to the thrust of the main goal.

Q: So you have a unity of story there?

MRS: You have a unity of time, place, and characterization. A play always has far more characterization than any pageant you could see. And I guess the primary difference you would say is story line, carefully constructed to disclose the conflict and its meanings. At least that's where I put it, and, people, its okay for them to argue about it.

Q: No, that's great.

SJP: Mark has written four or five outdoor dramas. He knows what he is talking about.

Q: I don't want to argue about it, but I am wondering that they don't achieve some of the same purposes. I mean there's a commemorative aspect; there's a celebratory aspect. You know what I mean?

MRS: Oh, yes, of course.

Q: So there is some overlapping of terms that we could use to kind of bridge the gap between those two terms, I mean. I mean I'm thinking of *The Lost Colony* and sometimes its describing pageant, and I think of the early versions definitely are more pageantlike.

MRS: No, the *New York Times* did a report on that one; look up the report.

Q: So, but I mean it is more pageantlike than the later versions.

MRS: Well, "pageantlike" is descriptive, and if you have an idea what a pageant is. Yes, it is historical events being portrayed, but the structure is vastly different. Although the display you see might look similar, you have spectacle, you have music, you have dialogue probably. So I don't find, I don't find it necessary to push them together. Maybe I misunderstood what you were saying. But the elements that are useful in storytelling in one form can be quickly adapted to another. It happens in all the experimental theories. But mostly we are, we are trying to create a particular impact that is centralized in play form rather than just the display. The importance is more than the display in the play.

Q: I have probably the dumbest question. Do most outdoor theatres, outdoor summer theatres, have policies about eating and drinking while they are watching the show? I speak as someone who really doesn't know. Like I am thinking the last outdoor drama I saw was not a historical drama; it was outside, *Hamlet*. Or the courtyard in Hamlet's castle and it had bleachers set up and it was at night and it was a retelling of the myths *Hamlet*'s based on for an audience who's listening to their history. On some level right? Being told that this is Danish, it's a Danish story, and just as the lights started to get a little bit dim in the story, everyone just started pulling out food. And this was the audience that you might imagine would go to any number of cultural events. There were a few kids there, not a whole lot. It might have been that they were tourists, but they were mainly a Danish audience. But they, the food was a very big deal, and I thought, Is that part of it, and are there policies for and against that?

RFF: Well, with the destination theatres, primarily the policy would stem from the fact that they do have concession stands and most of them, items purchased, I mean you do have popcorn and nachos and things.

Q: People bring in their dinners and, you know—

RFF: But, there are several companies that do preshow dinners there on the facility, but I don't know, with the destination theatres primarily there wouldn't be a situation where you would bring your food.

Q: Bring your picnic!

RFF: Yeah, there would certainly be theatres where those kinds of facilities were outside the house, where you may bring those things.

Q: Picnic tables, where you would bring your stuff and eat on the lawn, and then once you are in the theatre, you would sit down.

SJP: That's very common with Shakespeare festivals, but they play primarily to local audiences with only about three exceptions. There are sixty-four outdoor Shakespeares in the nation—only three of which are destination theatres—the rest of them play primarily to local audiences, and a great many of them encourage picnics. Lake Tahoe Shakes is one of them. There are two, two history plays that I know of that actually—boy, this is going to make you wince—two of them that actually serve meals during the performance.

Q: Like basketball, or dinner theatre.

SJP: And he [RFF] is going to see one next week: *Ramona,* in Hemet, California.

Q: You can go and buy a box dinner and go and sit on the grass and watch the show.

SJP: Very common in Shakespeare festivals, but not in history plays.

RFF: But most of the productions—not that there are many—but most of the productions that take place in the Forest Theatre across the street . . . actually most of those companies encourage people to bring food.

Q: Encourage to bring your dinner, yeah, bottle of wine some beer I mean that's I don't know. I just wondered like, it seems that there is some kind of expectation that, you know, you're not only watching a play but you are outside. Someone was talking about the other day being outside that it just becomes a different event and that no matter who the audience is they want to eat.

Q: It's also the Danes.

Q: And doesn't the New Globe in London . . . I mean they want to throw back to the time of Shakespeare, when you would actually be, you know, noshing on some hazelnuts or oranges. You know what I mean? I think in other words part of that is an attempt to say this is the way Shakespeare would have engaged his audience, talking back and heckling.

SJP: In my day at the IOD we often recommended that people who want to start history plays serve meals themed to the story before the play opens. So Young Abe Lincoln in Lincoln City, Indiana, would have what they call "rail-splitter dinner." My favorite was, you remember, *Old Four Eyes* in Medora, North Dakota? Teddy Roosevelt—*Old Four Eyes*—they no longer do that show, they do a musical revue now. I went out to see them ten years ago. And they're also down in a canyon, and on top of the canyon they serve a steak fondue dinner before the show. They've got these great big oil barrels and they fill the barrels with oil and they've got flame underneath the barrels. So the oil in the barrels gets real hot, and then they've got pitch forks, and they skewer steaks on these pitchforks, put them into the oil, and then you walk along to the barrels; they pull out the pitch forks and you take your steak, and people love it.

Q: That's going to make us hungry for dinner.

SJP: There are a lot of theatres that serve meals before the show. Most theatres—most history plays—do not encourage eating during the performance unless you want to bring in popcorn, that sort of thing. Shakespeare festivals are different.

Q: I was just curious because, actually it looked so interesting to me that the recommendations that you make, I mean the assessment, the feasibility studies that you do, wondering what kind of recommendations you make about front-of-house issues. How do you get them into the theatre? Out of [the] theatre? Eating? Drinking? You know?

MRS: Well, you have a big expense with the cleanup, unless you are very careful about how you handle the food—that includes the concession stuff at the intermission. So different theatres just handle it different ways. But the budget is what usually constrains. It's much easier to go through and pick up some paper cups, a napkin or two here and there. Instead of going through and picking up a lot of food junk. The cost is considerable. So that, that has to be figured in, but the individual company decides whether it wants a meal before, whether a lot of its funding came from restaurants up the street, in which case they probably won't serve any. I did serve a meal once, as well as deal with the companies that did. And it was for the opening of the play I was working in Kentucky, outdoor drama. We had another house; we had a number of people come through, a great number of invited dignitaries, because it was the opening of the play. And I went in to try to get something to eat and I got a piece of chicken since one of the people had been real nice and got us stuff from a Kentucky Fried Chicken place. We bought all of our stuff from the Kentucky Fried Chicken place and a place that specialized in Kentucky ham (and which I think was Virginia ham). But anyways, when I went in and sat down in the back, a fella came over and sat at the table, and I looked up and it was the face you see on the Kentucky Fried Chicken. The Colonel came in and sat with me, and there was not a piece of fried chicken on his plate; he had only ham.

SJP: Have we got the stories in outdoor drama or what?

Q: Scott, are you writing these down? Are you going to have a memoir?

MRS: I have to have something like this to remind me.

SJP: What I need to do is to sit down with Mark and pick his brain with a tape recorder and videotape it.

JM: Well, there's a start today, I guess. Does anybody have any other compelling questions? I would like to thank the panelists; this has been great.

"No Roof Except the Sky"

The Rise and Fall of Airdomes in American Popular Entertainment

Landis K. Magnuson

UPON THE OPENING OF W. F. Brinton's new airdome in the southeastern Iowa community of Washington early in the summer of 1908, the local *Evening Journal* heralded: "The great craze in the larger cities for the past several years during summer months has been open air games, exercises and performances of different kinds which has given rise to the construction of air domes, which have become so very popular in the larger cities that the theatres and indoor places of amusement of any merit close during the summer months and all enjoy the pleasant, mirthful and healthful summer breezes in the air domes."[1]

Built with an impressively ornate front facade (figure 1), the Washington airdome (like many others) was strategically located among businesses near the town square, in this instance only a short distance from the community gathering place of the local post office. In highlighting the development of such entertainment venues, the *Evening Journal* claimed that a general progression of airdome construction from larger to smaller cities was under way at the time, having moved in recent years from cities the size of Chicago to cities of "only twenty-five and thirty thousand inhabitants" to cities of "ten and fifteen thousand" to towns the size of Washington, which barely exceeded 4,250 in population at that time.[2] Each and every airdome built, boasted the local press, offered seating in the open air, which benefited "the general health of mankind, for after being shut indoors through the winter the health of every individual demands all the outdoor air possible in work or pleasure, hence from natural causes and the public good has the fad for the air domes sprung."[3]

Figure 1. Ornate front facade of the Washington, Iowa, airdome. Photo courtesy of the Museum of Repertoire Americana, Midwest Old Threshers, Mount Pleasant, Iowa.

Much of the rich history of airdomes must be gleaned from the depths of local newspaper accounts and the popular trade publications of the era. For example, the editorial page of *Billboard* in the fall of 1909 provides an optimistic, but certainly not prophetic, assessment: "The airdome is a branch of the amusement business that has come to stay." Although providing a rather romanticized view of the airdomes, the editorial does outline its chief characteristics:

> With the stage erected out-of-doors, and with no roof except the sky, and with the moon furnishing most of the light necessary, the airdome proved to be the ideal place to spend the evening, furnishing an opportunity to enjoy the entertainment without courting suffocation. With no expensive building to rent and vacant lots being cheap, the airdome immediately proved to be not only a more comfortable place of amusement, but an inexpensive one for the promoter. This is the reason why there will be more airdomes next summer, and they will be erected and conducted on a scale more elaborate.[4]

Contemporary accounts and historical overviews of the period establish the development and flourishing of airdomes from around the beginning of the twentieth century until the World War I era, perhaps reaching their greatest period of expansion a few years prior to 1910. Despite being a significant popular entertainment format, which flourished well beyond a single decade and continued in various levels of practice for decades to follow, only a scant amount of academic analysis and subsequent publication has taken place. Why? Perhaps it is because airdomes have been viewed as only a short-lived, second-tier entertainment practice. Possibly the phenomenon has been overshadowed by the major investigations during the past thirty-five years into other popular entertainment formats such as tent repertoire, circle stock, vaudeville, and touring stock ensembles. It simply may be that the story remains more difficult to recover. In response, this essay aims to expand significantly the story of airdomes, with particular emphasis on the performance offerings in the venues and, perhaps more important, to augment and integrate the existing visual record of this rarely discussed segment of popular entertainment.

Audiences enjoyed a wide offering of live performances in the airdomes, ranging from traditional repertoire companies to dramatic stock ensembles to vaudeville troupes and solo variety performers. This range of talent appeared, in large part, because airdomes frequently were owned and operated by entrepreneurs who controlled the local theatre venue (often referred to as the opera house), as well as the circuits that supplied the entertainment. Virtually every form of talent performing indoors eventually made a path to the outdoor airdomes. In addition, many airdome venues offered motion pictures, frequently in the combination of "moving pictures with illustrated songs,"[5] or even created an aggregate of vaudeville acts, motion pictures, and local-talent presentations.[6] An invaluable issue of the *Airdome Bulletin* dating from 1913, published at Stuttgart, Arkansas, outlines the apparent exclusive reliance of the local airdome on moving pictures. On Saturday, August 2 of that year, the headline motion picture was a Lubin special titled *The Guiding Light*, advertised as a "2-Reel Feature of Exceptional Merit." In addition to this was scheduled *An Equine Hero,* a comedy titled *A Mistaken Calling,* and the Edison drama *Little Girl Next Door.* Admission was set at five and ten cents, with the added incentive of a cash prize to be given away that evening.[7]

In the waning years of both airdomes and repertoire theatre during the Second World War, the practice of "picture circles"—namely circle stock operations based exclusively on showing sound movies—became popular. The low overhead present in running a picture circle most certainly attracted Jack and Nona Hart to such a venture in Arkansas in 1942. Distribution companies were known to offer for rent a 16-mm sound projector and a complete program of feature, short, and serial films for as little as $6.00.[8] Undoubtedly, some small touring outfits, in the 1940s and for many years previously, combined the keen interest in motion pictures found in remote areas with the availability of inexpensive rental units, and these groups "airdomed" by traveling with only canvas sidewalls, a projector, and a simple cloth screen.[9]

Numerous airdome circuits developed to supply and route entertainment, with the Crawford circuit, the Bell circuit, and the Olendorf circuit, all out of Kansas City, considered among the oldest and most prominent; however, airdome circuits too numerous to mention developed to provide the talent needed on a consistent basis.[10] For instance, in 1909 the McAdams circuit, headquartered in Dallas, supplied talent for airdomes in a total of thirteen cities in Texas and Oklahoma.[11] The following year marked the formation of the Missouri-Kansas Airdome Association, representing a dozen venues in this two-state region. Reportedly the burlesque wheels provided the model for the Missouri-Kansas airdome circuit, with *Billboard* explicitly stating that this circuit intended to operate on "a sort of a co-operative plan by which every manager of a theatre also owns a traveling company, which plays one week in his theatre and one week in each other theatre on the circuit."[12]

A handful of historians have made important initial inroads into the study of airdomes. One-time performer turned scholar William Slout, in his groundbreaking 1972 work *Theatre in a Tent: The Development of a Provincial Entertainment,* argues in a brief discussion that the success of amusement parks created by electric trolley companies around the year 1900 spurred the development of airdomes as a summer theatregoing event, in large part, because the venues remained close to home, often being situated in the local business district.[13] He notes that with a summer operation of no more than twenty weeks a year, a typical airdome facility consisting of a covered stage, open-air seating, and privacy created by a high board fence helped keep investment in such a venture under control. Slout further identifies that the initial reference to airdomes in the *New York Dramatic Mirror* dates from 1905 with information highlighting the Air Dome Theatre in Topeka, Kansas. This theatre, arguably the first airdome of record, opened on July 4 of that year with a vaudeville program, and the *Dramatic Mirror* reports, "From all appearances this little theatre will be the main attraction for the balance of the warm weather, as owing to its cool and airy construction, and with the promise of its first-class bookings, it will merit a capacity that will give promise of a big financial success."[14]

To his credit Jere Mickel bases his short 1974 analysis of airdomes in *Footlights on the Prairie* on personal experience as a patron of traveling shows, as well as eight years of professional touring with repertoire theatre companies. Somewhat vexing, however, is his heavy reliance on two summary articles by veteran performers published in *Billboard* decades earlier (and, more important, decades after the fact).[15] Mickel describes the airdome as normally consisting of "an area surrounded by a temporary wall of canvas, metal or wood without any roof covering, with the ground for the floor where the seats were placed. The stage at the back was a covered area along with off-stage areas and the dressing rooms all of which were masked from the audience, usually with canvas."[16] With a box office in front, the middle filled with rows of benches, these entertainment centers were often situated on a prominent vacant lot in a town's business district but at times were located at the outer edge of a community. Mickel claims that airdome capacity typically ranged from five hundred to fifteen hundred and that some airdomes employed an adjustable canvas roof to protect the audience in case of inclement weather.[17]

In point of fact, companies offering standard canvas products such as Columbus Tent and Awning of Ohio seized on the opportunity of protective coverings for airdomes and boasted of "All kinds of Tents, Airdome Tops and Canvas Goods," assuring them to be the best available.[18] Certainly, unseasonably cold conditions, and, more often, rainy weather, represented a considerable challenge to the success of the airdomes. It is not unusual to uncover reports of instances like that in June of 1908 at the airdome of St. Joseph, Missouri, where "almost constant rains throughout the week cut out all but a few performances."[19] The following year persistent rains prevented all but one or two performances by the North Brothers Stock Company at this very same venue.[20] Undoubtedly such experiences motivated managers to explore the financial and structural possibilities of providing some type of audience cover to help ensure that performances could go on.

More recently, theatre historian Richard Poole's review of route listings, covering the period from 1905 to 1915 as found in the major sources of *Billboard*, the *New York Dramatic Mirror*, and the *New York Clipper*, helps provide an understanding of the scope of the airdome movement throughout this nation and beyond.[21] Although his research is significant, presently only a compressed summary of his findings has made it to print.[22] During the decade under investigation, Poole reports discovering 439 airdome venues situated in thirty-six states, as well as Canada and France; the majority were found in Kansas, Oklahoma, Missouri, Texas, Illinois, Indiana, Ohio, and Pennsylvania. Poole argues that the airdome phenomenon developed out of an extensive Midwest theatrical circuit that had its start as early as 1893 and was controlled by the Kansas theatre impresario Lester M. Crawford. Poole further asserts that

Figure 2. Want ad placed by the Garden Airdome of Richmond, Indiana. Photo courtesy of the Museum of Repertoire Americana, Midwest Old Threshers, Mount Pleasant, Iowa.

the first airdome theatre likely was created by Crawford or by one of his four sons.[23]

The simple truth remains that the recovery of the story of airdomes is ongoing. Basic groundwork has been completed, but essential research remains. The study of airdomes, however, is particularly challenged by a paucity of print and photographic ephemera. Nevertheless, a variety of valuable examples hereby can be situated in context, the majority shared for the first time.[24]

Traditional Airdome Venues and Talent

A "Wanted" ad once placed by the Garden airdome of Richmond, Indiana (figure 2), reminds us that musical tabloid ("tab") shows and standard repertoire dramatic companies extensively played the airdomes. Such ensembles fit the venue well and were actively sought by managers. But a danger exists in concluding that such companies dominated these facilities to the exclusion of more prominent ensembles or that prestigious production troupes simply held no interest. Route listings in trade publications record the active scheduling in the airdomes of established stock companies, along with their traditional theatrical offerings. Consider, for example, that in late May and early June of 1909, Edward Doyle's Orpheum Stock Company satisfied those in attendance at Young's Garden airdome in Terre Haute, Indiana, with a collection of standard favorites of stock companies, including *The Garrison Girl; The Parish Priest; A Soldier of the Empire; The Little Church across the Way;*

Figure 3. Small handbill for the Van Dyke and Eaton Stock Company appearing at the St. Joseph [Missouri] Airdome. Photo courtesy of the Museum of Repertoire Americana, Midwest Old Threshers, Mount Pleasant, Iowa.

Sherlock Holmes, or The Sign of the Four; The Duke's Daughter; The Flower of the Mountain; College Chums; and *Two Orphans.*[25] Earlier in May 1909 Young's Garden airdome hosted the Herald Square Opera Company in performances of *A Trip to India; The Mascotte; Chimes of Normandy; Fra Diavolo;* and *The Moor's Bride.*[26]

Extant publicity and print evidence further supports that established stock companies actively performed in the airdomes. One example of such an event is a handbill for the St. Joseph, Missouri, airdome (figure 3), home we are told of the Van Dyke and Eaton Stock Company, featuring Helen Brandon.[27] A program entry for the Harvey Stock Company (figure 4) indicates that the company appeared in a production of *Alaska* at an unidentified airdome (likely Dubuque, Iowa) in July of 1910. An existing large herald for the Barton Stock Company (figure 5), measuring approximately fourteen by thirty inches, announces a week's stand at the Washington, Iowa, airdome introduced at the beginning of this essay.

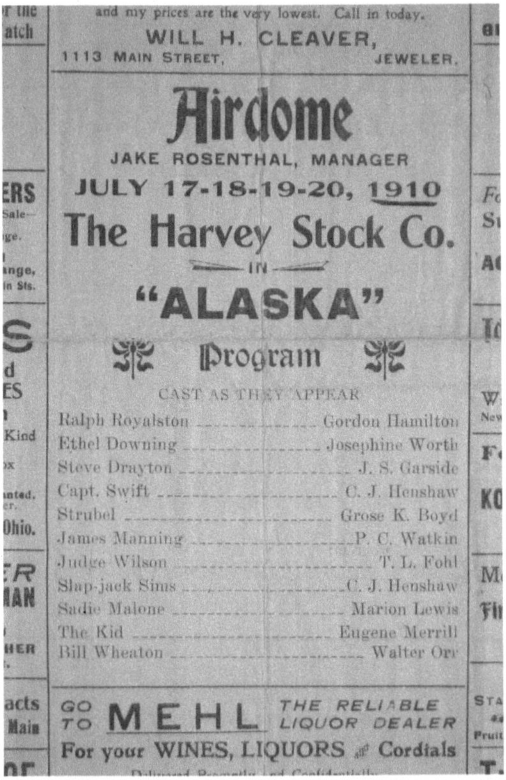

and my prices are the very lowest. Call in today.
WILL H. CLEAVER,
1113 MAIN STREET, JEWELER.

Airdome
JAKE ROSENTHAL, MANAGER
JULY 17-18-19-20, 1910
The Harvey Stock Co.
IN
"ALASKA"
Program
CAST AS THEY APPEAR

Ralph Royalston	Gordon Hamilton
Ethel Downing	Josephine Worth
Steve Drayton	J. S. Garside
Capt. Swift	C. J. Henshaw
Strubel	Grose K. Boyd
James Manning	P. C. Watkin
Judge Wilson	T. L. Fohl
Slap-jack Sims	C. J. Henshaw
Sadie Malone	Marion Lewis
The Kid	Eugene Merrill
Bill Wheaton	Walter Orr

GO TO MEHL THE RELIABLE LIQUOR DEALER
For your WINES, LIQUORS & Cordials

Figure 4. Portion of program for the Harvey Stock Company appearing at unidentified airdome (likely Dubuque, Iowa), July 1910. Photo courtesy of the Museum of Repertoire Americana, Midwest Old Threshers, Mount Pleasant, Iowa.

Figure 5. Large herald for the Barton Stock Company appearing at the Washington [Iowa] Airdome Theatre. Photo courtesy of the Museum of Repertoire Americana, Midwest Old Threshers, Mount Pleasant, Iowa.

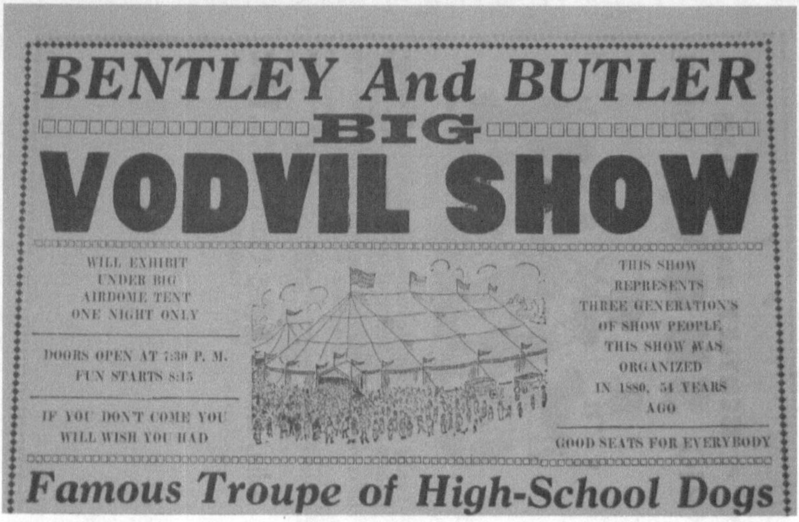

Figure 6. Portion of flyer for the Bentley and Butler Big Vodvil Show. Photo courtesy of the Museum of Repertoire Americana, Midwest Old Threshers, Mount Pleasant, Iowa.

Vaudeville companies and solo variety performers also toured extensively over the airdome circuits. A slate of entertainment offered at the new airdome in La Crosse, Wisconsin, once included (in addition to moving pictures) the eclectic lineup of Casey and Le Clair, Irish comedians; Arthur Abbott, English Coster singer; the Carson Brothers, Swedish athletes; the Three Pearce Sisters, singers and dancers; and E. C. Raymond, with illustrated songs.[28] A mid-May 1909 opening of the San Antonio airdome, headlined by the singer Dorothy Owen, also included the presentation of a three-person drama titled *Bess* and a blackface comedian named Jack Foster, as well as a skit presentation, motion pictures, and illustrated songs.[29]

While route listings and reports regularly provide lineups of variety artists performing in the airdomes, available publicity material can assist us to bring such performers and acts more fully to life. The Bentley and Butler Big Vodvil Show once featured a troupe of trained dogs (so-called High-School Dogs), and although a standard tent image is present on a flyer used by the company (figure 6), the copy informs us that the Vodvil Show will exhibit "under big airdome tent one night only"; a clear reference (although both a mixed publicity and grammatical message) to the use of canvas sidewalls and the remote possibility of a protective canvas covering during this 1934 season.[30] And even though the

Figure 7. Handbill for mentalist Ruth Grey, appearing at unidentified airdome. Photo courtesy of the Museum of Repertoire Americana, Midwest Old Threshers, Mount Pleasant, Iowa.

bold heading of a Ruth Grey handbill (figure 7) leaves little doubt that the mentalist would perform in an airdome for a single week, it is interesting to note the range of venues that Grey lists in the bottom right of this publicity item—from three weeks at the Kansas City Convention Hall, to seven weeks at the Lyric Theatre in Omaha, to five weeks at the Ft. Worth Vendome Theatre, to two weeks at the Evansville, Indiana, airdome. It is evident that the airdome offered a viable performance space to an assortment of companies and solo performers of the period, who freely moved through a variety of venues differing in style, size, and prominence.

Sparse photographic evidence and penny postcard images of airdomes further establish the range in scale and scope of these venues. An airdome on the smaller order could be found in Atchison, Kansas (figure 8), promoted as "Atchison's Joy Spot."[31] Signage claims high-class musical comedy and vaudeville, with the program changing nightly. Additional signage boasts Grace Hutchison "must be good" if she "plays the airdome." The airdome of Fayette, Missouri (figure 9), proves to be an accommodating venue with some nine rows of bleacher seating on both sides of a ground level of approximately twenty rows, complete with a

Figure 8. Photo of Atchison, Kansas, airdome, known as "Atchison's Joy Spot." Photo courtesy of the Museum of Repertoire Americana, Midwest Old Threshers, Mount Pleasant, Iowa.

Figure 9. Postcard image of Fayette, Missouri, airdome. Photo courtesy of the Museum of Repertoire Americana, Midwest Old Threshers, Mount Pleasant, Iowa.

Figure 10. Aerial photo of the Mitchell, Indiana, airdome. Photo courtesy of the Museum of Repertoire Americana, Midwest Old Threshers, Mount Pleasant, Iowa.

central isle.[32] The physical arrangement of this airdome must be considered classic; certainly an impressive venue in size and quality for a town barely exceeding a population of twenty-five hundred in 1910. Of special interest is the extensive paid advertising in the tradition of an opera house olio curtain, apparently painted on the back wall of the stage, as well as portions of the proscenium. A rare aerial photo of the Mitchell, Indiana, airdome (figure 10) succeeds in placing the long and narrow venue in relationship to the surrounding business establishments and the nearby residential area in a rapidly growing community, which doubled in size in the first decade of the twentieth century.[33]

In contrast to these relatively modest airdomes are considerably more substantial edifices, such as the impressive two-story Airdome Theatre of Danville, Illinois (figure 11), located in a city of nearly twenty-eight thousand at this time.[34] Although the Danville airdome appears to be situated in that community's business district, it does not seem to be in the immediate proximity of a legitimate theatre. Such combinations were frequent, however, as the airdome provided relief from heat and humidity during the summer months, and the adjacent indoor theatre could host performances in case of inclement weather. The large airdome of Fort Wayne, Indiana (figure 12), is representative of this configuration as it was located directly aside the Majestic Theatre within the urban business center of this bustling city of more than sixty thousand.[35]

Of particular importance is the image of a large airdome crowd

Figure 11. Postcard image of the Airdome Theatre, Danville, Illinois. Photo courtesy of the Museum of Repertoire Americana, Midwest Old Threshers, Mount Pleasant, Iowa.

Figure 12. Postcard image of Fort Wayne, Indiana, airdome, located next to the Majestic Theatre. Photo courtesy of the Museum of Repertoire Americana, Midwest Old Threshers, Mount Pleasant, Iowa.

Figure 13. Interior photo of crowd in the Beatrice, Nebraska, airdome, c. 1911. Photo courtesy of the Museum of Repertoire Americana, Midwest Old Threshers, Mount Pleasant, Iowa.

(figure 13) taken from the stage—reportedly in Beatrice, Nebraska, circa 1911, and located next to the town's opera house—which provides a unique glimpse into some of the audience amenities of the period.[36] One can note the typical practice of raked bleacher seating to the right and to the left of the ground level, as well as the prominence of a control booth or projection hut at the rear of the venue. In addition one can surmise significant electric lighting present. If not electrified, airdomes most likely utilized gravity flow, white gas units, or possibly even kerosene. Little is known about particular audience conveniences offered in airdomes, but obviously they ranged considerably, based on the size and stature of the venue. The Marvel airdome in Winston-Salem, North Carolina, must be viewed as moderate in size by seating eight hundred but could well be considered high end in audience comforts, as it offered a smoking room, as well as a refreshment parlor, plus music provided at performances by a resident orchestra. The manager, M. O. Mead, also boasted of specially designed interior decorations.[37]

Canvas Sidewalls Only

While most airdome locations established a degree of permanence by erecting substantial sidewalls of board or metal (which could lead to

Figure 14. Exterior photo of canvas-sided airdome used by the Fontinelle Theatre Company. Photo courtesy of the Museum of Repertoire Americana, Midwest Old Threshers, Mount Pleasant, Iowa.

greater appointments and elegance), some venues sported only a cloth surround by choice. An undated photo of the Fontinelle Theatre Company (figure 14) provides a unique glimpse of a canvas-sided airdome.[38] What can we view in this rare image? We are able to see a young boy, complete with straw hat, approaching a colorful striped entrance adorned with an American flag flying prominently overhead. The canvas sidewalls are a minimum of seven feet tall, and we also are able to detect that one corner of the airdome is conveniently anchored by what appears to be a utility pole. Various scenarios can explain why the Fontinelle Company has been captured airdoming while utilizing only canvas sidewalls. Certainly the company might have discovered the relative ease of transporting and erecting a performance space consisting primarily of only a canvas enclosure. Or perhaps the lower initial cost, as well as reduced expenses in using and maintaining a foldable barrier, were of importance. And it should not be overlooked that on the most basic of levels, airdoming allowed this company to play in towns without a permanent theatre structure.

The photo of the Chick Boyes Players (figure 15) performing in Hebron, Nebraska, during the 1920s offers an uncommon view of the in-

Figure 15. Interior photo of canvas-sided airdome used by the Chick Boyes Players in Hebron, Nebraska, c. 1920s. Photo courtesy of the Thayer County Museum, Belvidere, Nebraska.

side setup of a canvas airdome. Certainly the canvas proscenium topped with an eye-catching American flag, along with the bleacher seats located in the left of the image, are consistent with the type and quality of equipment used by Chick Boyes's troupe while touring at this time under canvas. Unquestionably these elements come from their own tent equipment. However, two styles of wooden benches are present—one folding and the other clearly more permanent and substantial—which suggest a variety of sources being pressed into service.

It is not clear if the Fontinelle or the Boyes companies used canvas venues for the touring of a single bill, or perhaps three-night stands, or week rep, or even circle stock. On an industry-wide basis, it is very probable that canvas airdomes were used at some time, in some place, for all of these touring methods. Support, in part, for this assertion comes from the use of soft-sided airdomes by Henry and Ruby Neal in the 1930s, who together operated circle stock in Colorado for the entire year using a combination of theatres and open air settings. *Bill Bruno's Bulletin* reports that "seats and stage are temporary in each town and only the sidewall and stage covering are moved, making the daily setup very easy."[39] With bulky seating and stage equipment situated in each of the towns on the circuit, transporting the canvas components was done with relative ease. These veteran troupers once boasted of only one airdome performance a year on average falling victim to rough weather conditions during a three-year span.[40] Although it is possible that only six to eight months annually were spent airdoming because of their northern Colorado location, it still stands as a remarkable feat in the creative use of a canvas airdome.[41]

In addition to reasons some companies chose to use only canvas sidewalls, on occasion necessity required an ensemble to turn to this performance arrangement following a tent "blow down" and the devastation left in its wake. Trade publications of the period frequently report the destruction caused by severe thunderstorms or tornadoes, as when *Bill Bruno's Bulletin* reports in June 1929: "The M and M Players, management of M. L. Mitchell, suffered the entire destruction of their top at Stickney, S.D., on Tuesday night of last week during a sixty-mile-an-hour wind storm, which closely resembled a tornado in violence." The account concludes by stressing that "the top was torn to ribbons and the company finished their engagement in a make-shift airdome, using only a side wall, stage platform and proscenium."[42] In similar fashion we learn of the Bob Grandi tent show losing its top during a windstorm at Mart, Texas, in 1929. We are informed that "enough of the dramatic end was salvaged, together with sidewall, to allow the company to open at Clifton on Monday night under an improvised airdome."[43] By salvaging key components of the tent operation, most importantly the canvas sidewalls, a company could continue performing while awaiting a new canvas top to replace the damaged one.

Mickey Lacey, a veteran of the waning years of repertoire theatre, recalls one afternoon with Bisbee's Comedians in Russellville, Kentucky, soon after the onset of a severe storm. Lacey relates that as the chaos of the event unfolded, he grabbed a "jumping" quarter pole close to the concession stand in an attempt to stop it:

> At that point I was remembering what my dad and some old timers had always said, "Just about one of the safest places to get to was under the stage." I was seriously thinking of heading that way; however, I didn't quite make it. I really don't remember if I was still trying to hold that pole in place or if I had made the decision to head to the stage. It didn't matter! I remember looking up and seeing that big, heavy canvas go over.
>
> Poles and stakes were flying through the air like projectiles. Ropes were popping right and left and a terrible sounding moaning of wind was present. Then, just like that, it was over! I found myself wading my way out from under the concession stand. Ice, syrup, popcorn aplenty. We all started

> calling names and listening for answers. I called Dad's name, but heard no answer. I was scared to death of the worst. However some[one] yelled, "Here he is!"[44]

Although photos of the damage caused by this storm are yet to be found, a representative example of such havoc can be seen in a blow down suffered by the Chase-Lister company (figure 16), reportedly at Harlan, Iowa, circa 1929. In these battles between nature and canvas, typically the tent top bore the brunt of the damage while the sidewalls escaped tearing or could be repaired in a reasonable amount of time. Above all, the rule of the day required an expedient return to performing, and that often involved airdoming.

End of an Era

The *New York Times* records in the summer of 1910 both the literal collapse of a venue in New Jersey and perhaps a symbolic forecast of the eventual fall of the popularity of airdomes. Under the title "Airdome Falls in Paterson/Scare in Nearby Streets When Open-Air Theatre Collapses with a Crash" we learn:

> The Airdome, an open-air theatre at Main and Ward Streets, collapsed to-day. No one was injured. The building was put up about three years ago, but it lasted only a short time as a playhouse, owing to litigation which is not yet settled.
>
> People living along Lee Place got a scare when the building came down with a crash, smashing fences in the rear of their houses and noisily carrying down telephone wires.
>
> The police say that boys have been chopping away the lower beams of the building, and that this had probably weakened it.[45]

While a single cause is apparent for the collapse of this venue, a variety of reasons have been offered for the demise of the airdome practice. These reasons center primarily on the performance offerings of the companies, as well as on the impact of changing technology and pressures concerning the real estate value of the venues. Will Locke, a veteran rep and stock actor, in his noted *Billboard* article titled "Gay '90s Airdomes Ace Summer Spots for Repsters," believes that the loss of the freshness of the experience brought about the decline: "For several summers the airdomes flourished but consistent with the ancient philosophy that very often the thing that seems to be a great success contains the germs of its final undoing. So, like all new projects, when the novelty wore off, the

Figure 16. Photo of Chase-Lister company blow down, reportedly at Harlan, Iowa, c. 1929. Photo courtesy of the Museum of Repertoire Americana, Midwest Old Threshers, Mount Pleasant, Iowa.

airdomes began to decline. An unforeseen angle of the project was that continuous stage offerings throughout the summer, gave patrons a surfeit of that kind of entertainment."[46]

Jere Mickel adopts E. L. Paul's position (from a 1943 *Billboard* summary) that the musical tab shows, tremendously popular in the indoor houses and subsequently booked heavily into the airdomes, seemingly never caught on in these outdoor venues. Whether this position is supported by existing evidence remains to be seen. Unquestionably, tab companies were a staple of airdome programming. In 1909 both the College Girl Musical Comedy Company and the similarly sounding Matinee Girl Musical Comedy Company maintained extensive touring schedules.[47] Also on record are tab companies that specifically spoofed the airdome performances of classical opera groups such as the Boston Ideal Opera Company.[48] This touring ensemble once undertook an open-ended series of performances, with change of bill semiweekly, at the Leavenworth, Kansas, airdome.[49] Mickel also follows Will Locke's position that eventually the novelty of continuous theatrical fare—whether dramatic, tab, vaudeville, or some combination thereof—created by the indoor theatre season, directly followed by the summer airdome season, simply wore thin. But suggesting that the demise of the airdomes came about primarily because of extending popular theatrical fare throughout the calendar year seems insupportable. If such theatrical offerings remained viable in the indoor venues, it does not stand to reason that the same fare singularly would cause the fall of the airdomes. Certainly a greater complexity of factors is at play here. Mickel concludes by asserting that one positive impact of the significant decline of airdomes was the "turning [of] the rep shows toward the use of the tent as a summer theater."[50]

Other historians have staked differing positions concerning the demise of the airdomes. William Slout argues a far more practical and business-oriented position, emphasizing that increasing street noises from automobiles and the rising values placed on midtown locations forced such open-air summer theatricals to an end. Richard Poole offers a comprehensive analysis, placing nearly equal emphasis on a variety of factors, ranging from the development of air-conditioning to the increasing popularity of motion pictures, to poor management of the airdome venues, to transportation advances lessening rural isolation, to fatigue over poor weather, as well as the novelty of the experience giving way. Certainly the invention of air-conditioning and its negative impact on the practice of airdomes cannot be underestimated and requires a more complete analysis. Ironically, a 1911 report on the addition of a large cooling plant to the Princess Theatre in St. Louis is striking in that it boasts of the elimination of "hot and impure air" while promising a cooling experience: claims once exclusively emphasized by the airdomes.[51]

Charles R. McAdams Jr., manager of the McAdams airdome circuit, saw a singularly bright future for airdomes in 1909, declaring (perhaps, in part, for his own benefit) that they had "come to stay and that they are not a transient fad—a whim of to-day and a memory of to-morrow."[52] We now know that performances in airdomes could not be maintained at the level viewed by McAdams a short way into the twentieth century and that the use of airdomes was reduced even by the time this nation turned its attention to the hostilities of the Great War. In a relatively short time airdomes were reduced to the realm of nostalgia, and submissions to the "Do You Remember Away Back When" column found in *Bill Bruno's Bulletin* frequently sported entries that recalled the height of the airdome phenomenon, including various airdome circuits and locations. For example, during early summer in 1929 the column asked readers if they could recall when "Airdomes flourished throughout the midwest and provided the work during the summer months now offered by the tent show?"[53]

Such recollections of a seemingly forgotten practice notwithstanding, airdomes proved to be a viable performance practice for years, often for companies that had fallen on difficult times. In the same year that *Bill Bruno's Bulletin* asked if readers could remember the time when airdomes flourished, Horace Murphy reported making a great success of an "airdome stock . . . built on the plan of the old-time airdomes of the midwest," situated some two miles outside the city limits of Phoenix, Arizona.[54] Also in 1929 noted rep manager Frank Winninger removed his company from the road when theatre bookings were refused to him, and he built an open-air theatre on the lot adjoining his home at Schofield, Wisconsin. Upon opening his new venue, Winninger refused to acknowledge the history of airdomes by name or by inference and claimed the idea was "entirely his own." He christened the new performance space "Eventide," and it proved to be a success for multiple seasons.[55]

During the Depression era and beyond, airdome practice continued and in many cases proved highly successful. For example, one unique arrangement of airdome circles was utilized in the early 1930s by Cal and Florence Berry out of Maryville, Missouri. According to trouper Robert La-They, this couple established three one-week circles, complete with a separate company that rotated through each of the circuits, thus requiring a new bill to be learned only once every third week. These units toured with canvas sidewalls and used the stage portion of a "dramatic-end" tent as an essential element.[56] Charles Berkell, a well-known Midwest rep performer, operated an airdome during the 1932 season in Davenport, Iowa, and later in that challenging decade, Henry and Ruby Neal in Colorado, as previously outlined, regularly turned to airdome venues to maintain year-round trouping between indoor dates and open-air performances.[57] Even as late as spring 1943, *Billboard* columnist E. F. Hannan swears to know of two tent repertoire companies of the "swarms" planning to tour the Southwest "who are going to use side walls only" because of the difficulty of obtaining suitable complete canvas units during the war years.[58] The economic exigency of the war years proved once again the sustaining power of the practice of airdoming. In light of the use of airdomes as late as World War II, perhaps the assessment of Charles McAdams decades earlier that airdomes "are and will remain successful" carried more than a well-intentioned entrepreneurial boast. Perhaps the allure of "no roof except the sky" did, in fact, have more staying power than the historical record has previously understood or appreciated.

Notes

1. The early practice of using two words *(air dome)* or even a hyphenated plural *(air-domes)* gave way over time to the standard use of *airdome* and *airdomes.*

2. U.S. Census Bureau, *Thirteenth Census of the United States: 1910*, "Iowa: Chapter 1—Number of Inhabitants," Table 2, www2.census.gov/prod2/decennial/documents/36894832v2ch05.pdf (accessed March 31, 2008). The 1910 population of Washington was 4,380 (609).

3. *Washington (Iowa) Evening Journal*, June 5, 1908, 3.

4. *Billboard*, Sep. 25, 1909, 16.

5. As found at the Abbert airdome of Terre Haute, Indiana; see the *New York Dramatic Mirror*, June 5, 1909, 8.

6. As found at the airdome of Palestine, Texas; see the *New York Dramatic Mirror*, June 26, 1909, 8. Years later such a practice became known as a "Vaude-Pic Combo"; see *Billboard*, June 8, 1940, 26.

7. *Airdome Bulletin* [Stuttgart, Arkansas], Aug. 2, 1913, 1. This particular issue of the *Airdome Bulletin* newsletter is very likely the sole surviving one and is listed as volume 1, number 36. My special thanks to Russell Baker of the Arkansas History Commission/State Archives for his assistance in securing it.

8. *Bob Feagin's Bulletin*, April 8, 1942, 2. Ad for the Eastin Film Company of Colorado Springs, Colorado, and Davenport, Iowa, found in *Billboard*, April 4, 1942, 27. *Bob Feagin's Bulletin* (January 1941 to May 1942) was a Midwest theatrical newsletter that succeeded *Bill Bruno's Bulletin*.

9. See Landis K. Magnuson, *Circle Stock Theater: Touring American Small Towns, 1900–1960* (Jefferson, NC: McFarland, 1995), 208. Confusion can arise from the use of the term *airdoming* as used in the present study with that which was strictly associated with tent companies. According to Russell Kittle, airdoming for a company performing in a tent involved the practice of taking down the sidewalls and enlarging the seating capacity by erecting poles along the sides at some distance from the edge of the tent top and placing the side canvas along these poles. Tent-show managers used this version of airdoming to increase capacity and to improve air circulation. See Russell D. Kittle, "Toby and Susie: The Show-Business Success Story of Neil and Caroline Schaffner, 1925–1962." 2 vols. (PhD diss., Ohio State University, 1969.)

10. Both the naming and spelling of prominent circuits do vary. For example, E. L. Paul notes the Crawford circuit and the Bell-Olendorff circuit (*Billboard*, Nov. 13, 1943, 31); Will Locke only mentions the Bell-Orendorf circuit (undated *Billboard* article, n.p.); Jere Mickel states that the Bell and Ollendorf circuit and the Crawford circuit out of Kansas City were "the best known" (Jere C. Mickel, *Footlights on the Prairie* [St. Cloud, MN: North Star Press, 1974], 51); Richard Poole states "among the most prominent being Kansas City's Bell and Olendorf and the Crawford Circuit" ("Airdomes," in *The Cambridge Guide to American Theatre*, 2nd ed. [New York: Cambridge University Press, 2007], 58). Elsewhere I have made mention of the Bell-Ballard-Olendorf circuit and the Crawford circuit (Magnuson, *Circle Stock Theater*, 43). Various entries in the "Do You Remember Away Back When" column in *Bill Bruno's Bulletin* in 1929 and 1930 highlight the Bell circuit run by W. W. Bell, as well as the Bell-Olendorf circuit. It is important to note that often Bell and Olendorf are united in reports as a single circuit but not always. Furthermore, circuits virtually too numerous to mention existed. For example, circuits cited in the *New York Dramatic Mirror* in 1909 include, but are not limited to, the McAdams circuit in Texas and Okla-

homa (May 29, 1909, 6); the Iowa-Illinois circuit (June 19, 1909, 5); and the Airdome Amusement Company circuit headquartered in Washington, Pennsylvania (July 31, 1909, 13). Circuits mentioned in *Billboard* include, but are not limited to, the Sherman circuit in Missouri, Illinois, and Indiana (July 3, 1909, 45) and the Eastern Theatrical Exchange (July 29, 1911, 19). *Bill Bruno's Bulletin*, published in Kansas City between 1928 and 1930, and 1935 and 1940, was a popular trade publication for Midwest rep and circle stock companies.

11. *New York Dramatic Mirror*, May 29, 1909, 6. Cities in Texas included Dallas, Waco, Fort Worth, Cleburne, Gainesville, and Denison; cities in Oklahoma included Oklahoma City, Tulsa, Bartlesville, Enid, El Reno, Shawnee, and McAlester.

12. *Billboard*, Feb. 5, 1910, 16.

13. William L. Slout, *Theatre in a Tent: The Development of a Provincial Entertainment* (Bowling Green, OH: Bowling Green University Popular Press, 1972).

14. *New York Dramatic Mirror*, July 15, 1905, 6. Additional reports on the early weeks of the Air Dome Theatre in Topeka identify successful two-a-day performances in the afternoon and evening but the venue being challenged when faced with strong counterattractions in the area.

15. See Mickel, *Footlights on the Prairie*. Mickel relies heavily on two *Billboard* historical summary articles in his account: E. L. Paul, "The Airdomes Come and Go," *Billboard*, Nov. 13, 1943, 31; and Will H. Locke, "Gay '90s Airdomes Ace Summer Spots for Repsters," *Billboard*, undated clipping, n.p. The Locke article can be located in an Al Pitcaithley scrapbook housed at the Museum of Repertoire Americana, Mount Pleasant, Iowa. Despite effort, no date or page number(s) have been established. The Locke article is clearly from *Billboard*, and based on font and style characteristics, it appears to date from the early 1940s.

16. Mickel, *Footlights on the Prairie*, 212.

17. Reports of seating capacity vary and generally range from two hundred to two thousand. While the largest airdome capacity appears to have been in St. Louis at four thousand, capacity numbers frequently reported in the trade publications are eight hundred, fifteen hundred, and two thousand.

18. *New York Clipper*, July 9, 1910, 547.

19. *New York Dramatic Mirror*, July 4, 1908, 11.

20. *New York Dramatic Mirror*, July 24, 1909, 13.

21. Special thanks to Richard Poole for allowing me to draw from his paper "Spectacular Novelty: The Airdomes of Iowa, 1905–1915," presented at the Theatre History Seminar at the Museum of Repertoire Americana, Mount Pleasant, Iowa, 1991.

22. See Poole, "Airdomes," 57–58.

23. According to Poole ("Spectacular Novelty"), Lester M. Crawford created the first airdome circuit in Kansas, and the owner/management of the Air Dome Theatre in Topeka, at the very least, maintained business connections with Crawford. It is not established at this time, however, if Crawford himself founded the Topeka airdome of note.

24. In the interest of full disclosure, my own discussion of airdomes in *Circle*

Stock Theater contributes several pages of text and three photo images to the scholarly record. In this article the image of a canvas-airdome setup by the Chick Boyes Players in Hebron, Nebraska, in the 1920s is courtesy of the Thayer County Museum in Belvidere, Nebraska. All remaining examples of paper ephemera and visual images are courtesy of the Museum of Repertoire Americana, Mount Pleasant, Iowa. Special thanks to Martha Hayes and Michael Kramme of the Museum of Repertoire Americana for their cheerful and unstinting assistance.

25. *New York Dramatic Mirror,* June 19, 1909, 5; *New York Dramatic Mirror,* June 26, 1909, 8.

26. *New York Dramatic Mirror,* June 5, 1909, 8.

27. A "Do You Remember Away Back When" entry in *Bill Bruno's Bulletin* (Jan. 2, 1929, 8) once asked, "When Van Dyke & Eaton played the airdome in St. Joseph, Mo.?"

28. *New York Dramatic Mirror,* July 24, 1909, 13.

29. *New York Dramatic Mirror,* June 5, 1909, 8.

30. Although it is certainly possible that the phrase "Will Exhibit Under Big Airdome Tent One Night Only" could refer to the tent theatre practice of placing the sidewalls out at some distance from the edge of the tent top (as discussed in note 9 above), it is highly unlikely in this situation. Erecting a tent for a single performance in 1934 and feeling the need to increase capacity during the Depression era simply doesn't ring true. As such, all indicators point toward the use of a traditional airdome setup in this instance, with the possible use of a protective canvas top.

31. U.S. Census Bureau, *Thirteenth Census of the United States: 1910,* "Kansas: Chapter 1—Number of Inhabitants," Table 2, www2.census.gov/prod2/decennial/documents/36894832v2ch05.pdf (accessed March 31, 2008). The 1910 population of Atchison was 16,429 (664).

32. U.S. Census Bureau, *Thirteenth Census of the United States: 1910,* "Missouri: Chapter 1—Number of Inhabitants," Table 2, www2.census.gov/prod2/decennial/documents/36894832v2ch09.pdf (accessed March 31, 2008). The 1910 population of Fayette was 2,586 (1089).

33. U.S. Census Bureau, *Thirteenth Census of the United States: 1910,* "Indiana: Chapter 1—Number of Inhabitants," Table 2, www2.census.gov/prod2/decennial/documents/36894832v2ch04.pdf (accessed March 31, 2008). Between 1900 and 1910 the community of Mitchell grew in population from 1,772 to 3,438 (539).

34. U.S. Census Bureau, *Thirteenth Census of the United States: 1910,* "Illinois: Chapter 1—Number of Inhabitants," Table 2, www2.census.gov/prod2/decennial/documents/36894832v2ch04.pdf (accessed March 31, 2008). The 1910 population of Danville was 27,871 (469).

35. U.S. Census Bureau, *Thirteenth Census of the United States: 1910,* "Indiana: Chapter 1—Number of Inhabitants," Table 2, www2.census.gov/prod2/decennial/documents/36894832v2ch04.pdf (accessed March 31, 2008). The 1910 population of Fort Wayne was 63,933 (539).

36. U.S. Census Bureau, *Thirteenth Census of the United States: 1910,* "Nebraska: Chapter 1—Number of Inhabitants," Table 2, www2.census.gov/prod2/

decennial/documents/36894832v3ch1.pdf (accessed March 31, 2008). The 1910 population of Beatrice was 9,356 (39).

37. *New York Dramatic Mirror,* June 19, 1909, 5.

38. Letterhead used prior to 1910 for "The 3 Fontinelles" identifies that at that time Robert and Harrietta were running a tightwire act, certainly with assistance in some form by their young child, Nina. This canvas airdome could date from such an early period because the faint image of special circus-style performance equipment (perhaps trapeze rigging?) can be seen directly to the right of the front entrance. Robert C. ("Pop") Fontinelle maintained a lengthy career in tent rep and circle stock, and *Billboard* featured his preparations for the 1942 tent season (touring to an established territory in Iowa and Missouri) as being his fiftieth year as a manager. Fontinelle reportedly started as a manager for an indoor circus in 1892 (*Billboard,* April 4, 1942, 41). An issue of *Winging It* identifies that the Fontinelle Stock Company was based out of St. Louis: "The show's territory was Missouri with an occasional foray into northern Arkansas and southern Iowa. Each winter, with just the family members, the show did circle stock, generally based out of St. Louis. The family kept the show on the road from 1908 to 1942" (*Winging It* [spring 2005]: 2). *Winging It* is the official newsletter of the National Society for the Preservation of Tent, Folk, and Repertoire Theatre, based at the Museum of Repertoire Americana, Mount Pleasant, Iowa.

39. *Bill Bruno's Bulletin,* June 3, 1937, 15.

40. *Bill Bruno's Bulletin,* June 24, 1937, 1.

41. For additional discussion of canvas airdomes see Magnuson, *Circle Stock Theater,* 207–10.

42. *Bill Bruno's Bulletin,* June 20, 1929, 2.

43. *Bill Bruno's Bulletin,* Aug. 1, 1929, 2. On one occasion Bill Bruno recalled Bob Grandi's building the Crystal airdome in Joplin, Missouri, and placing his own stock company in it to perform (*Bill Bruno's Bulletin,* Feb. 13, 1930, 8).

44. *Winging It* (Summer 2006): 7.

45. *New York Times,* June 26, 1910, 5.

46. *Billboard,* undated clipping, n.p. As discussed in note 15, this article is located in an Al Pitcaithley scrapbook housed at the Museum of Repertoire Americana, Mount Pleasant, Iowa.

47. *New York Dramatic Mirror,* May 29, 1909, 6.

48. For example, Morris B. Streeten's Musical Comedy Company presented travesties on popular comic operas during performances at Frank Rich's airdome in El Paso in 1909 (*New York Dramatic Mirror,* July 17, 1909, 14).

49. *New York Dramatic Mirror,* July 10, 1909, 12.

50. Mickel, *Footlights on the Prairie,* 53.

51. *Billboard,* July 29, 1911, 19.

52. *New York Dramatic Mirror,* June 19, 1909, 5.

53. *Bill Bruno's Bulletin,* June 13, 1929, 10.

54. *Bill Bruno's Bulletin,* Aug. 22, 1929, 4.

55. *Bill Bruno's Bulletin,* July 25, 1929, 8; *Bill Bruno's Bulletin,* June 5, 1930, 3.

56. Robert La-They, audiotapes to author, Feb. 14, June 26, 1986; letter to author, Oct. 2, 1987. For more information on "dramatic-end" tents see various discussions in Magnuson, *Circle Stock Theater;* and Slout, *Theatre in a Tent.*

57. *Billboard,* Sep. 17, 1932, 22; *Bill Bruno's Bulletin,* June 3, 1937, 15.

58. *Billboard,* May 8, 1943, 26.

Rail-izing the Nation along Lake Michigan

The *Wheels a-Rolling* Pageant

Jane Barnette

IN 1948 CHICAGO hosted a fair to celebrate railroad history, the centerpiece of which was a "colossal pageant" depicting the pivotal role that the railroad industry played in westward expansion and "social progress" of the United States.[1] Financed by nearly forty separate railroad companies, the pageant was an unabashed opportunity to seize the spotlight for train culture's twilight performance.[2] A scant three years after World War II, railroad lines were once again desperate for passenger business, after experiencing a boom in passenger and freight services earlier in the 1940s. By the end of this decade, public opinion supported the building of national highways, made possible by the Federal Highway Act of 1944, and railroad companies were "hard hit by the competition from cars and planes and burdened with an inventory of equipment all but worn out by hard use during [the war]."[3] More significant, as fellow train culture scholar Kyle Gillette argues, "the Holocaust made trains synonymous with industrialized death." In the postwar worldview the locomotive was seen by many as a "dehumanizing conveyor belt that carried millions to concentration camps in Germany, Poland, and Austria."[4] To combat this perception, U.S. railroad companies banded together to forge an interactive summer-long fair to commemorate the centenary of train service through Chicago, "the acknowledged railroad capital of the nation."[5] Typical of the fair culture that Chicago epitomized in its 1893 Colombian Exposition and held on the same grounds as its 1933 Century of Progress Exposition (in Burnham Park, alongside Lake Michigan), the stories being told at the *Wheels a-Rolling* transportation history pageant were defiantly nostalgic while simultaneously idealizing the future.

Much of the performance-related literature about this event concentrates on the serendipitous visit that Walt Disney made to the Chicago Railroad Fair in its first year, during which he was apparently inspired to create his own theme park, Disneyland.[6] Other relevant scholarship theorizes the ways that fair culture capitalized on the voyeuristic appeal of exoticized Others. Robert Rydell, for example, demonstrates how world fairs were "triumphs of hegemony," insofar as they successfully promoted the corporate status quo.[7] What has yet to be articulated are the ways that the railroad pageant performance manipulated the public to create a train-centered vision of the United States.

In what follows I examine the staging of the *Wheels a-Rolling* pageant of the Chicago Railroad Fair to consider how the traditionally interior consumer experience of train travel was staged outdoors. Following the tradition of David Nye, who queries the ways "Americans narrated their place in the world and imagined their position in history in technological terms," my discussion offers insights into how Americans in the Midwest were encouraged to imagine their national, regional, and colonial past through the outdoor (rather than indoor) lens of train culture.[8] Drawing from an extant program for the 1949 fair as my primary evidence, along with the critiques provided by cultural historians like Nye and William Cronon, I use the pageant as a case study to query how fair organizers hoped to inspire a surrogate, train-centered version of U.S. history, even in the wake of a burgeoning automobile culture.[9]

Defining Genres

Wheels a-Rolling bears a striking resemblance to earlier railroad pageants held on fairgrounds, as the program recognizes with the attribution, "adapted from a pageant play by Edward Hungerford."[10] Hungerford, who died shortly after the Railroad Fair opened, earned a reputation as an impresario of train culture for his prolific (and irrepressibly positive) articles and books about locomotion. As the official historian of the Baltimore and Ohio line, he was commissioned to oversee the company's centennial fête in 1927. His brainchild, the *Fair of the Iron Horse*, became the blueprint for two pageants that would, in turn, provide the basis for *Wheels a-Rolling*. In 1933, at Chicago's Century of Progress exposition, Hungerford staged *Wings of a Century*, but "it was left . . . for the New York World's Fair of 1939 to bring it to the full form of an operatic presentation," through the inclusion of music (composed by Kurt Weill), with song and dance.[11] It was this pageant, *Railroads on Parade*, that solidified Hungerford's role as a "poet of the streamliners," leading the Newcomen Society (American Branch) to boast of his "outstanding contribution to the progress of Pageantry in America."[12] So cutting-edge was this New York railroad pageant, in fact, that it featured voice-overs amplified from a booth located under the audience for all the sound, including that of the actors and a twenty-five-piece orchestra.

The genre of pageantry is not synonymous with that of outdoor drama. Although recent scholarship attests that "there is no single definition of exactly what constitutes an outdoor drama," the Institute of Outdoor Drama (IOD) locates its origins in North Carolina, with the development of "symphonic drama."[13] Paul Green, who coined the term *symphonic drama* to describe his outdoor performances, made the following distinction in his 1946 preface to *The Lost Colony:*

> [CRITIC:] Do you call it a pageant or a play?
> [GREEN:] A play. For it tells a story, and the characters are individuals—at least I mean them to be—not types, as is usually the case in masques and pageants.[14]

The distinction is a matter of degree, to be sure—both the symphonic plays classified as outdoor drama and its predecessor, the historical pageant, utilize music, dance, and narration to educate the public about local and national history—but it is a significant difference nonetheless. As *The Lost Colony*'s first director, Samuel Selden, attests, Green "broke from the form [of pageantry] in one important way: he limited the time covered by the drama and focused principal attention of the spectators on a small group of characters."[15] In contrast, the historical pageant was known for its broad sweep of history, its immense spectacle, and for focusing on ideas, industries, or cities rather than on individually developed characters.

In some regards, though, symphonic drama shared common philosophical goals with historical pageantry. Noting that Green's dramaturgy was artistically superior to the pageants of the early twentieth century, Green's mentor, Frederick Koch, nonetheless referred to *The Lost Colony* as part of the pageant tradition, insofar as "pageantry is the most democratic of all the arts. In it all may have a part—poets, players, designers, singers, and dancers. I know of no better way toward an imaginative—a spiritual expression of our American life than by this popular dramatic form."[16] Likewise, pageant pioneer Percy MacKaye envisioned community pageant-making as "the ritual of democratic religion," the very basis by which citizens could enact their ideal political and social world.[17] In both of these outdoor performance contexts, the production process (as well as product) has the potential to unite and give voice to a community. Providing such opportunities for citizens to contribute labor and ideas toward how their community represented itself was radical indeed for early twentieth-century Americans.

Following this idealism to decidedly different goals was Edward Hungerford, who represented railroad businesses rather than private citizenry. As he reminded his fellow Newcomen Society members, his railroad pageant was about "*education*—visual education of a high sort, if you please—although we prefer to think of ourselves as offering entertainment, entertainment of a high order, we always hope, but entertainment that sends an audience of several thousand folk out of our theater on its heels, chattering, smiling, content, and, whether they know it or not, possessed of a knowledge of our American railroad, its workings and its position in the social scheme of the land that they have not before possessed."[18] Hungerford believed the spectators of railroad pageantry—whether they recognized it or not—were being reminded of the role train culture played "in the social scheme of the land," emphasizing its ongoing relevance in their community and in the nation at large.

Pageant Goals and Geography

Wheels a-Rolling ran four times daily, lasting approximately seventy-five minutes and featuring at least 150 human performers, "eighty horses and other animals," and fourteen scenes of transportation history, represented by historic as well as contemporary train engines chugging across the stage.[19] The pageant narrated transportation history chronologically, starting in 1673 with a prologue, "Indian Trails and Waterways," and ending with 1949, "Modern Transport."[20] Accompanied by two narrators, a five-member chorus, and a small orchestra (all amplified over a loudspeaker), *Wheels a-Rolling* featured a parade of trains, horses, bicycles, and automobiles that attracted family audiences by offering edification alongside entertainment. As the Chicago Railroad Fair's president, Lenox R. Lohr, put it: "By dramatizing instead of preaching, by making every exhibit a novelty in entertainment as well as education, the railroads have graphically driven home a realization of how much they mean in our national economy and what miraculous progress has been accomplished in rail transportation since its inception only a little over a century ago."[21] Noticeably absent from this depiction of "miraculous progress," however, was any recognition (let alone representation) of the role the rails played overseas as "the most destructive machine of the Holocaust"—instead, the pageant presented U.S. train culture without reference at all to the role its European counterpart had played in the recent war.[22]

As suggested by the repetition of the word *progress,* at the heart of the Railroad Fair was the then decades-old rhetoric of the Progressive Era (a period typically dated between 1890 and 1920).[23] Narratives of progress sought to "naturaliz[e] the technological transformation of the United States so that it seemed an inevitable and harmonious process," recasting the railroads as heroes instead of villains (or winners instead of losers) in the story of industrialized America.[24] The chronological design of the pageant—a logical choice, given railroads' insistent linearity—reinforced this story of inevitable progress by showcasing primitive locomotive designs replaced by (and in some cases alongside) new streamlined diesel trains. "Such contrasts . . . were intended to show how far railroads had advanced."[25] So long as the comparisons were limited to rail transportation, the narrative was successful—at the 1939 New York World's Fair, however, Hungerford and Weill's pageant was overshadowed by General Motors' Futurama exhibit, which boasted a miniature world of superhighways and automobiles as seen from an airplane. In this panorama of a future 1960 American landscape there were no trains (and no railroad tracks) at all.[26]

Nearly a decade later, without competing exhibitions from automobile makers, U.S. railroad companies seized the opportunity to present a nostalgic version of the familiar progressive narrative. By locating the fair in Chicago, the capital city of railroading, organizers surrounded fairgoers with train culture well before they reached Burnham Park. The city was not known only for being "the link that bound the different worlds of east and west into a single [rail] system"—even rapid transit in Chicago was visibly rail-based, since most of the early electric train-cars ran on elevated tracks.[27] More specifically, building the Railroad Fair on the same grounds as the Century of Progress Exposition, where Hungerford's earlier pageant *Wings of a Century* was also performed, reminded visitors of the triumph of modern science heralded there in 1933.

The pageant was staged on the south side of the fair, close to the Illinois Central tracks that were refashioned to showcase famous trains like the diesel-powered "Train of Tomorrow" sponsored by General Motors. From the main entrance, spectators had to either walk the mile-long stretch of fairgrounds or catch the "Deadwood Central," a narrow-gauge train that cost ten cents to ride and ran between the north and south ends of the fair. Admission to *Wheels a-Rolling* was sixty cents, roughly equivalent to five dollars in 2007 in terms of purchasing power.[28] The amphitheatre for the pageant had an initial capacity of five thousand in 1948; when the fair reopened in 1949, the seating was expanded to hold six thousand at each of the four shows that ran daily.

Seated in long benches in a grandstand, spectators faced a predominantly flat stage with at least two railroad tracks running parallel to the waterfront of Lake Michigan.[29] Massive concrete wings framed the pageant, providing both a proscenium-arch theatricality and the "panoramic perception" that Wolfgang Schivelbusch theorized as the precinematic train-window gaze of seeing the world in motion, framed by a machine.[30] These tall freestanding concrete slabs were unmistakably modern in design, an aesthetic that contrasted sharply with the earlier chronology of railroad development. They also served as semiborders of the pageant performance itself, directing the audience's eyes to the action taking place between them to partial exclusion of the other possible vistas. Although part of the train tracks extended beyond the wings on both sides, the main action was understood to occur between them. Additionally, spectators could see (and perhaps hear) the lake behind the stage, an effect that further distanced them from their mid-twentieth-century reality of skyscrapers and roadways.

By contrasting the parade of machinery against the backdrop of Lake Michigan the pageant engaged a metaphor so familiar it was virtually archetypal to mid-twentieth-century Americans: the symbolism of the machine in the garden.[31] The Railroad Fair organizers, facing the growing irrelevance of train travel, sought to rekindle the awe that seeing locomotive power alongside naturally produced motion had once inspired. As part of the attempt to conjure the past, the penultimate page of the 1949 fair program demonstrates the pageant's attention to perceived authenticity by listing the transportation equipment by name and offering the dates each machine was first used in the United States, as well as indicating whether the vehicle represented onstage was an "original" or a "replica." For brevity's sake I will address in detail three of the fourteen scenes described in the program, as representative of the overall story of transportation history promoted by this pageant. Taken together, scene 2 ("The Iron Horse—1829–36"), scene 8 ("Santa Fe—1878"), and the epilogue ("Modern Transport—1949") reveal how flexible and selective history could become when rendered through the eyes of train culture. To forge such a collective memory "is a process that depends crucially on forgetting," as Joseph Roach suggests. Like other outdoor pageants meant to celebrate a community's history, the performance can be seen as a surrogate for the authentic.[32]

Pageant Scenes and Stories

Although technically the third scene in the pageant, "The Iron Horse" was the first scene to showcase rolling stock, featuring replicas of the earliest American locomotives, the Best Friend of Charleston and the Tom Thumb (both first operated in 1829), as well as an original of the De Witt

Clinton (first used in 1831). The highlight of this scene was the race between the steam-powered Tom Thumb locomotive and a horse-drawn car. At each of the four daily performances, the "gray mare" powering the car would win the race, reminding audiences of just how primitive these earliest locomotive engines were—and thus, by default, how advanced the modern streamlined diesels were in comparison.[33] Although in this "epic race" Tom Thumb loses to horse power, the pageant program assures patrons that during this phase "as the John Hancock [1838 original], the Atlantic [1830 replica] and the LaFayette [1837 replica] add new records in the conquest of space, America's first railways begin to reach out across the nation."[34] By this logic, as train travel becomes faster, more and more tracks are laid, in turn drawing new settlers and businesses. This depiction of railroad development conquering (supposedly) uncivilized land was central to the foundational narratives of the United States.

Speed and distance were two essential benchmarks for assessing train performance, leading nineteenth-century critics to characterize the sweeping cognitive changes associated with their increased potential as the "annihilation of space and time."[35] Once considered the fastest way to travel, horse-drawn cars were quickly becoming outpaced by a steam-powered machine—thus, space and time themselves seemed to have been utterly destroyed. In other words, "this depiction of its effects [that space and time had been annihilated] resulted from the fact that the railroad's motive forces could not be comprehensibly connected to visible natural forces, such as the animal, wind, or water power that generated pre-industrial motion."[36] If not powered by a visible natural force, then how did those locomotives run? To witnesses of early trains, "the railroad struck many as a symbol of everything evil about industrialization" and seemed to be powered by malevolence itself.[37] Perceiving railways in such negative destructive terms was clearly at odds with the foundation narrative the fair (not surprisingly) preferred to embrace: that of locomotive power as a creative enabling force rather than one of obliteration and ruin.

Also sanitized in what was considered the high point of the pageant by Walt Disney, the Santa Fe–sponsored eighth scene evoked the American Southwest as a mixture of "romance and refinement" and "rough and tumble." Even the Santa Fe tracks are described in the pageant program as "ribbons of steel," juxtaposing the more familiar characterization of the rails as cold and metallic with the feminine "ribbons," suggesting decoration rather than devastation. This performance of incongruity nevertheless achieving harmony became more evident still through the pageant's depiction of "Spanish senoritas, charros, padres,

Navajos, prospectors, roustabouts and can-can girls [who] await the arrival of the first train. Arriving travelers, popeyed as they behold the wonders of a new world, are served by pretty girls, who add a note of romance and refinement to the rough and tumble towns of the old Southwest."[38] Although not identified by (brand) name, the civilizing female force described above was recognizably that of the Harvey Girls, waitresses who served tables of passengers and railroaders in Fred Harvey's chain of restaurants along the Santa Fe tracks.[39] The remarkable mixture of social classes along this route ultimately did embrace the "clean, businesslike, and efficient" Harvey House identity.[40] Arguably, the Harvey hotels operated under the same basic goals as the fair itself: to provide "predictable quality, safety, and every civilized amenity."[41] In short, both the Harvey chain and the Chicago Railroad Fair envisioned themselves as moral compasses of the untamed Southwest.

From other perspectives, however, the early public reaction to the western spread of train development was far from harmonious. Although the pulse of social attitudes is always difficult to measure, it appears that Americans resented the intervention of railroad speculators, since "railroads transformed settlement from an individualistic process to a centralized corporate practice." One of the turning points in the public's perception of railroads occurred in 1879, when a displaced settler sued the Santa Fe Railroad and the Supreme Court ruled in favor of the Santa Fe. This milestone case "amounted to official recognition that the railroad foundation narrative was falsified by the actual workings of the bureaucracy and the legal system."[42] In other words, before the turn of the century, Americans were already aware of the striking disconnect between the railroad's promises (of promoting settlement and creating communities) and the reality of living under its control. Furthermore, far from the amicable bonding implied by the group described as prospectors and roustabouts (among others), the relationship between transient railroad workers and western settlers was rife with tension. In particular, the caricature implied by the mixture of "Spanish senoritas," charros, padres, and can-can girls can hardly be overlooked. Assuming that by "padres" the fair meant priests or men of the cloth, and keeping in mind the bawdy nature of the can-can dance (not to mention the sexuality implied by the hot-blooded señoritas), it is quite a stretch to imagine this group peacefully gathering to await the arrival of the Santa Fe. While it is certainly true that the American Southwest boasted a more ethnically hybrid culture than elsewhere in the nation, significantly, it was "the American railroad and railroad systems [that] brought together Indian, Hispano, and Anglo peoples for the first time in a modern and modernizing setting."[43] In so doing, however, the western expansion of the railroad also brought "an entirely new class of people into the regions they traversed," and the tension between these classes and ethnicities was palpable.[44]

The striking disconnects between public perceptions of the rails and the fair's depiction of the rails were perhaps most evident in the final scene of the pageant, "Modern Transport." Whereas fair organizers were aware of the waning influence of trains in the shadow of the automobile, they nevertheless attempted to depict a seamless vision of railroad dominance. As they admit in the opening pages of the 1949 program, "Interweaving [all the attractions] is the unending evidence of the basic part the railroads are ready to play in America's economic and social progress in the future as they have done so effectively in the years now closed." In this final scene of the pageant, human actors were easily overshadowed by the locomotive display, in the hopes of reigniting the passion for railroading in spite of the midcentury craze for automobile transportation. The same concrete slabs that had directed spectators' gaze throughout the pageant now also functioned as blinders, blocking out the reality of the railroad's failure to be "the very lifeblood of our Nation," suggesting instead that the American train continued to play a leading role in the narrative of contemporary transportation.

The irony of this vision is unmistakable, given the fact that many (if not most) attendees drove to Burnham Park by automobile. Within the confines of the fairgrounds, organizers argued, visitors were able to experience "actual, personal participation" instead of attending "as a mildly interested spectator."[45] Through the embodiment of train culture, organizers hoped that audiences would be viscerally transported back in time to the age of the locomotive, as rendered by the railroad companies and the *Wheels a-Rolling* pageant.

Taking spectators on this particular journey in a postwar, automobile-driven context was quite a challenge. Whereas the rest of the fair offered opportunities to experience railroads from inside the trains, with few exceptions most audience members viewed the pageant from the grandstands, as an exterior event.[46] Certainly doing so was easier design-wise than attempting to recreate the interior experience of riding on a train (especially for thousands of spectators at a time), but might there have been an ideological payoff to the choice to stage the pageant outdoors? After all, the technological power—the annihilation of space-and-time effect—could most easily be appreciated from the perspective of onlookers rather than passengers. From the exterior vantage, spectators could appreciate the size, speed, and power of the railroad as a grander, even epic, story.

Within what Michel de Certeau has described as the "bubble of panoptic and classifying power" of train interiors, passengers are cut off from their localized contexts and communities and nudged into individual speculation.[47] For the thousands of spectators who watched *Wheels a-Rolling,* though, the outdoor experience was meant to be more communal and less private. Such outdoor displays of train culture like Hungerford's historical pageants "erased the enormous social tensions and environmental problems the railway system had created."[48] This was the remarkable feat that the Railroad Fair accomplished: to use the narrative of progress to look backward instead of forward. For, as Karal Ann Marling has argued, "when the trains of the future were introduced, the real emphasis . . . fell on the past—on the culture of railroading that the automobile had all but eradicated."[49] Hosting the fair on the same grounds as the Century of Progress exhibition, and staging the pageant on the lakeshore, enabled this sleight-of-hand by reminding fairgoers of earlier fair narratives and isolating the spectators' view.

Notes

1. Curtis L. Katz, "The Last Great Railroad Show," *Trains* (Aug. 1998): 63.

2. The fair's organizers recognized that railroads were no longer the dominant mode of transportation: "With The Chicago Railroad Fair of 1949, . . . we herald the start of a second century of rails into the sunset; we, at the same time, are forcibly reminded of the assets we have to meet our destiny" (Chicago Railroad Fair program, 1949, n.p.).

3. Karal Ann Marling, "Disneyland, 1955: Just Take the Santa Ana Freeway to the American Dream," *American Art* 5 (Winter-Spring 1991): 181. Although Congress passed the Federal Aid Highway Act in 1944, it would take until 1956, under President Eisenhower's leadership, for the interstate initiative to have enough federal funding. "Interstate Highway System," Wisconsin Historical Society, www.wisconsinhistory.org/archstories/late_roads/interstate_system.asp (accessed May 31, 2008).

4. Kyle Gillette, "Stages of Locomotion: The Space and Time of Railway Travel in Modern European and American Theater" (PhD diss., Stanford University, 2007), 129–30.

5. Katz, "The Last Great Railroad Show," 60.

6. See Marling and her thorough bibliography for more on Disney's fascination with the Chicago Railroad Fair. Railroad historian and archivist Curtis Katz has written extensively about this fair, but his meticulous reconstructions lack analyses of the pageant (or the fair) as performances.

7. See Robert W. Rydell, *All the World's a Fair: Visions of Empire at American International Expositions, 1876–1916* (Chicago: University of Chicago Press, 1984), 2. See also Rydell's *World of Fairs: The Century-of-Progress Expositions* (Chicago: University of Chicago Press, 1993).

8. See David E. Nye, *America as Second Creation: Technology and Narratives of New Beginnings* (Cambridge, MA: MIT Press, 2003), 5.

9. William Cronon, *Nature's Metropolis: Chicago and the Great West* (New York: Norton, 1991).

10. Chicago Railroad Fair program, 1949, n.p.

11. Edward Hungerford, *Setting History to Music: A Newcomen Address* (Princeton, NJ: Princeton University Press, 1939), 11.

12. Ibid., 8. As the Newcomen Society notes in its preface to Hungerford's address, it is named after Thomas Newcomen, the British engineer who invented the steam engine. Created in England after the First World War, the American branch of this society aimed to "succeed in sharing with America a strengthened inspiration to continue the struggle towards a nobler Civilization—through wider knowledge and understanding of the hopes, ambitions, and deeds of leaders in the past who have upheld Civilization's material progress. As we look backward, let us look forward" (preface to Hungerford, *Setting History to Music,* n.p.).

13. Carolyn D. Roark, "'Live! In the Canyon': Historical Pageantry as Community-Builder in the Paso del Norte," *Americana: The Journal of American Popular Culture (1900–present)* 6, no. 1 (Spring 2007): www.americanpopularculture.com/journal/articles/spring_2007/roark.htm (accessed May 31, 2008); Institute of Outdoor Drama, "Outdoor Drama Facts," www.unc.edu/depts/outdoor/media/media/facts.html (accessed May 31, 2008).

14. Quoted in William J. Free and Charles B. Lower, eds., *History into Drama: A Source Book on Symphonic Drama, Including the Complete Text of Paul Green's "The Lost Colony"* (New York: Odyssey Press, 1963), 120.

15. Quoted in ibid., 126.

16. Quoted in ibid., 136.

17. Quoted in David Glassberg, *American Historical Pageantry: The Uses of Tradition in the Early Twentieth Century* (Chapel Hill: University of North Carolina Press, 1990), 171.

18. Hungerford, *Setting History to Music,* 17 (Hungerford's emphasis).

19. Ward Allan Howe, "Rail Notes: More New Trains for Summer Runs," *New York Times,* June 12, 1949.

20. Chicago Railroad Fair program, 1949, n.p. In the first year of the fair the pageant ended with "the arrival of the *Pioneer Zephyr* at A Century of Progress," or a depiction of Chicago in 1933. When the fair reopened in 1949, however, the finale had been rewritten to showcase a more modern tableau (Katz, "The Last Great Railroad Show," 65).

21. Quoted in Ward Allan Howe, "Railroads Put on Their Own 'World's Fair,'" *New York Times,* Aug. 22, 1948.

22. Gillette, "Stages of Locomotion," 129.

23. For more on the Progressive Era see Steven J. Diner's *A Very Different Age: Americans of the Progressive Era* (New York: Hill and Wang, 1998).

24. Nye, *America as Second Creation,* 6.

25. Ibid., 201.

26. David Nye, *Narratives and Spaces: Technology and the Construction of American Culture* (New York: Columbia University Press, 1997), 126.

27. Cronon, *Nature's Metropolis,* 91. When the Railroad Fair opened (July 1948), the Chicago Transit Authority had just begun operating. In October of 1947 the CTA united two previously operational companies, the Chicago Surface Lines (formed in 1914) and the Chicago Rapid Transit Company (formed in 1924). See "CTA Overview," Chicago Transit Authority, www.transitchicago.com/about/overview.aspx (accessed Jan. 6, 2009).

28. Lawrence H. Officer and Samuel H. Williamson, "Purchasing Power of Money in the United States from 1774 to 2007," MeasuringWorth, http://measuringworth.com/calculators/ppowerus/ (accessed May 31, 2008).

29. The number of railroad tracks in use for the pageant stage is not clear—Marling states that there were two sets of tracks, but Ward Kimball states in a more recent interview that there were three. For the Kimball interview see "Walt's Family & Friends—Interview with Ward Kimball," http://disney.go.com/disneyatoz/familymuseum/exhibits/familyfriends/wardkimball/index.html (accessed May 31, 2008).

30. Wolfgang Schivelbusch, *The Railway Journey: The Industrialization of Time and Space in the 19th Century,* new edition (Hamburg: Berg, 1986), 62.

31. See Leo Marx, *The Machine in the Garden* (Oxford: Oxford University Press, 1965). David Nye's *America as Second Creation* has been described as a reworking of Marx's highly influential study.

32. Joseph Roach, *Cities of the Dead: Circum-Atlantic Performance* (New York: Columbia University Press, 1998), 2. As Roach maintains, all performance functions in some ways like surrogacy—since performance "stands in for an elusive entity that it is not but that it must vainly aspire both to embody and to replace" (3).

33. Chicago Railroad Fair program, 1949, n.p.

34. Ibid.

35. For more about the application and origins of the annihilation of space and time, see Schivelbusch, "Railroad Space and Railroad Time," in *The Railway Journey;* and Michael Freeman, *Railways and the Victorian Imagination* (New Haven, CT: Yale University Press, 1999).

36. Gillette, "Stages of Locomotion," 38.

37. Ibid.

38. Chicago Railroad Fair program, 1949, n.p.

39. Marling, "Disneyland, 1955," 183. Another significant incongruity here is the fact that the Santa Fe scene (featuring the Harvey Girls) is said to take place in 1878 in the fair program, but Fred Harvey did not start hiring waitresses as "Harvey Girls" until 1883, when he fired his entire team of black waiters because they had gotten into "a midnight brawl" (Lesley Poling-Kempes, *The Harvey Girls: Women Who Opened the West* [New York: Paragon House, 1989], 42). Significantly, virtually all the women hired to serve as Harvey Girls were white.

40. Poling-Kempes, *The Harvey Girls,* 55.

41. Marling, "Disneyland, 1955," 184.

42. Nye, *America as Second Creation,* 178–79.

43. Pablo Mitchell, *Coyote Nation: Sexuality, Race, and Conquest in Modernizing New Mexico, 1880–1920* (Chicago: University of Chicago Press, 2005), 2.

44. Nye, *America as Second Creation,* 184. In particular, as Nye observes, the Santa Fe Railroad historian described the "drifting railroaders [as having] gained a reputation as a boastful, rough-speaking, hard-living, immoral lot."

45. Chicago Railroad Fair program, 1949, n.p.

46. According to one of his leading animators, Ward Kimball, Walt Disney's favorite experience at the Railroad Fair was when he got to play the engineer on the Santa Fe train in the *Wheels a-Rolling* pageant (Marling, "Disneyland, 1955," 184). In addition, in terms of interior railway experiences, fairgoers could ride the Deadwood Express and eat in dining cars.

47. Michel de Certeau, "Railway Navigation and Incarceration," in *The Practice of Everyday Life,* trans. Steven Rendall (Berkeley: University of California Press, 1984), 111.

48. Nye, *America as Second Creation,* 202.

49. Marling, "Disneyland, 1955," 185.

Mormon Pageants as American Historical Performance

Martha S. LoMonaco

MORMON PAGEANTS are dramatizations of important episodes of American history that have been largely ignored by people outside of the Mormon faith. These pageants, outdoor historical dramas, are produced every summer as an evangelical, informational, and celebratory mission of the Church of Jesus Christ of Latter-Day Saints (LDS). There are seven pageants sanctioned by the Church, and all but one, an Easter pageant based on biblical text, dramatize personalities and events in Mormon history as they relate to the larger history of the United States. The productions are free of charge, are held in enormous outdoor amphitheatres that can accommodate thousands of spectators, and are performed from ten days to one month between June and August. All can be described as "symphonic dramas of American history," which is the phrase Paul Green used to describe *The Lost Colony* and subsequent outdoor historical dramas that meld historic personages and events with dramatic storytelling filled with music, movement, and pageantry.[1] They also dramatize the historical events on or near the sites where the events actually occurred so that audiences can "walk on hallowed ground" and have history "made real and alive to them," which the Institute of Outdoor Drama (IOD) considers a principal ingredient in the success of the genre.[2]

The pageants provide an alternative view of nineteenth-century U.S. history that challenges traditional narratives. Mormons were commonly depicted, along with Native and African Americans, as the feared "other" who, through their unusual lifestyle and religious practices, were perceived as threats to the morality and stability of the emerging nation. They aroused hostility and suffered persecution from their inception as a new religious community in the late 1820s, but anti-Mormon prejudice was not solely based on religion. As historians Leonard J. Arrington and Davis Bitton point out, for Mormons "'religion' encompassed much more than it did for their contemporaries. . . . Religion included not only theology and a standard of morality but also an eschatology, an economic philosophy, and a goal of community-building that inevitably meant political and economic tension with their neighbors."[3] E. E. Ericksen attributes "Mormon group consciousness and group morality" to their reluctance to assimilate into the larger community, while nonbelievers feared the economic competition and political domination that these sizable groups of Mormons, who "voted as a bloc," wielded particularly in rural areas.[4] There also was a shared revulsion for a religion that challenged the widely accepted values held by more traditional Christians, who believed that "civilization was founded on a basic commitment to Christianity."[5] This fear and loathing caused LDS adherents to be characterized by polemicists as a "mass of human corruption," "deluded fanatics," and "the dregs of society," among other slurs, and their beliefs to be "superstitious, disgusting, and repellent," as well as "a monstrous evil." Verbal denigration was often accompanied by physical abuse, which ranged from "threatening to shoot cattle, whip Mormons who resisted, demolish houses, or kill Mormons who sought redress; stealing or destroying property; burning, razing, or otherwise destroying houses and mills; whipping and beating or tarring and feathering men; turning people out of their homes; and 'driving' groups of Mormons to new locations."[6]

After the LDS published its official sanction of polygamy in 1852, local and regional persecutions expanded to a national scale that involved the federal government and the military. The new Republican Party adopted a "radical, reformist platform" at its 1856 convention that included "an explicit connection between polygamy and slavery" that it termed "the twin relics of barbarism" in the U.S. territories. The party's call to abolish these "relics," which it also dubbed the "nation's two peculiar domestic institutions," quickly escalated to a national cause célèbre that resulted, at various times, in open warfare, congressional legislation, and a continuing struggle over governance of the Utah territory.[7] The Mormon leadership formally and publicly proclaimed the cessation of polygamous practice in 1890, and after prolonged efforts to attain statehood, Utah finally became a state in 1896. Yet renegade bands of fundamentalists who refuse to acknowledge the 1890 decree still adhere to polygamous lifestyles in the twenty-first century, a practice that tends to tar all Mormons with the same negativist brush despite vociferous condemnation from the LDS. Polygamy aside, Mormons, who continue to function in the same group-oriented, community-centered manner that provoked nineteenth-century hostilities, still experience a troubled relationship with many Americans. The sociologist Rodney Stark, who has written extensively on Mormon communities, remarked as recently as 2005 on the continuing prejudice against Mormons, even among religious scholars. "I continue to be astonished that my colleagues—who would *never* utter anti-Semitic, anti-Catholic, or even anti-Muslim remarks—unselfconsciously and self-righteously condemn the Latter-day Saints." Stark insists that "it is time we did better," but outreach remains largely the province of the LDS, through various media, including the historical pageants, to change the tide of public opinion.[8]

The pageants may, in fact, be gaining wider audiences beyond the Mormon community, particularly in the wake of the 2007–2008 presidential campaign of Mitt Romney, which promoted an increasing national interest in Mormons and Mormonism. Audiences are still predominantly composed of Mormons, however, who attend and frequently perform in the pageants as family holiday experiences. Although potential converts are welcomed (cards are placed on every seat for audience members to request a free copy of *The Book of Mormon,* and smiling ushers offer additional information about the Church), the larger aim of the pageants is education, commemoration, and celebration. Mormons desire acceptance as legitimate participants in the forging of the American nation, and their "symphonic dramas of American history" are as historically and theatrically rich as more populist tales of national evolution, such as those depicted in the venerable trio of North Carolina outdoor dramas, *The Lost Colony, Horn in the West,* and *Unto These Hills.* The fact that the pageants are also musical theatre performances is equally historic since theatre, dance, and music have been an integral part of Mormon life and religious culture since the Church's founding. That this was true in an era when most religious denominations, as well as many local municipalities, viewed theatre and dance as tantamount to devil worship makes this aspect of American cultural history even more fascinating.

The LDS has ascribed the name *pageant* to what would otherwise be categorized as an outdoor historical drama for numerous reasons. The term *pageant* has deep historical roots in two specific types of theatre: the medieval mystery plays of western Europe and the early twentieth-century civic pageants performed throughout the United States. The mystery plays, adaptations of Bible stories that were written to familiarize the illiterate masses with the Old and New Testaments and to inculcate Christian doctrine and morality, were often referred to as pageants because of the wagons that served as mobile stages for the individual plays. Since the Mormon pageants also focus on religious teaching, particularly of the life of Christ and how he figured in the creation of Mormonism, the linkage to historical Christian dramatic traditions is desirable. The other type of pageant, which commemorates the history of a municipality and honors the people who built it in what David Glassberg terms "a dramatic public ritual through which the residents, by acting out the right version of their past, could bring about some kind of future social and political transformation," is equally salient since the Mormons special-built numerous towns to function as religious communities and safe harbors for their growing numbers of adherents.[9] Since their faith is largely based on family lineage, the LDS consider contemporary members direct descendants of the Nauvoo homesteaders who, indeed, sought the social and political transformation that would occur in Utah. Today the pageants function to ensure the continuance of Mormon communities and to help those outside the faith understand how Mormon family values and lifestyles are congruent with those of the larger American culture. Hence, their pageants combine religiosity with civic pride and celebration in a manner that both incorporates theatrical antecedents and distinguishes these from the more conventional narratives of the outdoor historic drama movement.

The most representative and dramatically noteworthy of the pageants is held in Nauvoo, Illinois, which, for Mormons, is one of the three most important "hallowed grounds" in the country. Nauvoo was developed by the Mormon First Prophet and Founder Joseph Smith as the American Zion, where the faithful would join in community to await the Second Coming of Christ. Historians of Mormonism emphasize the importance of place in the development of the faith, particularly since the chosen sites were so unusual in the Judeo-Christian tradition. Douglas Davies notes that since "the history of the world has been marked . . . by the emergence of groups dedicated to their religious ideals and seeking to manifest them within communities established as separate from others," Joseph Smith was not unusual in his desire to create a new city for his adherents. What was unique, however, was his pronouncement that Christ would return not to Jerusalem, as many Christians assume, but "to a sacred place in North America."[10] Smith initially believed that place would be Independence, Missouri, and then Kirtland, Ohio, but continued persecution led him to Nauvoo, on the banks of the Mississippi River, where he laid out a city plan and established a thriving community of twelve thousand before he was assassinated in 1844. Within two years after his death, the Mormons fled Nauvoo in the wake of continuing harassment and embarked on their thirteen-hundred-mile exodus west, where they would finally settle in their permanent American Zion in Utah's Salt Lake Valley. Nauvoo, however, remains the town that the Prophet, as Smith is known throughout the LDS, built and is thus a place of pilgrimage to walk the "hallowed ground" and celebrate his endeavors through dramatic pageantry.

Nauvoo is now largely a restored village and tourist destination, which becomes an extended theatre stage for the entire month of July, with nightly performances of the pageant being supplemented in the daylight hours by a lengthy preshow of nineteenth-century residents at work and play plus six historic vignettes performed on or near the actual sites where the dramatized events occurred. There are an additional five Broadway-style musicals that are lightly flavored by history and performed by bubbly, young Mormon missionaries, many of whom are seeking degrees in musical theatre at Brigham Young University. The serious historical drama, however, occurs in the newly revised pageant and in the six vignettes that are outtakes from the pageant. This scheme allows the main event to be a compact seventy-five-minute performance, while audience members interested in learning more can attend the separate vignettes, which feature the same actors offering more extended portrayals of their pageant characters. All performances rely heavily on reclamations of the type of theatre, music, and dance performed in the 1840s by the Nauvoo Dramatic Society, the Nauvoo Brass Band, and the ever-popular community dances, which were held in private homes and social halls.

The new historically based performances are a direct result of an unusual intervention by LDS central authority in Utah. With the exception of the *Hill Cumorah Pageant*, which premiered in 1937 (coincidentally, the same year as *The Lost Colony*), most of the pageants are local affairs, wholly created and performed as Mormon missionary community theatre. Although the LDS gives some technical support, as well as advertising on its Web site, there is no formal church involvement. However, plans to celebrate the 200th anniversary of Smith's birth in the city he founded, which included the reconstruction and dedication of the Nauvoo temple, reputed in its day to be the most magnificent building in middle America, propelled Church headquarters to become actively engaged. David Warner, director of the Music and Cultural Arts Division of the LDS, was given the assignment in August 2004, eleven months before the dedication of the temple and the pageant's opening night, to create an entirely new show that would more accurately reflect the history and spirit of Nauvoo as it was in the 1840s. The previous pageant, *The City of Joseph*, which had been performed successfully for twenty-nine years, was largely a song-and-dance extravaganza, described by one longtime observer as a "frolic in the park without much depth to it."[11] Warner described the three objectives in the remaking of the pageant: to tell the story of Nauvoo using true stories from journals and the historical record; to use hymns and American folk songs and dances of the period as the basis for the music and choreography; and to ground all aspects of the production, from scenography to the style of writing, in the mid-nineteenth century. "When we remember, in terms of recollect, we also re-member ourselves into this community to connect directly to our history," he explained. "We feel that we cannot move forward if you don't gather up the past and bring it with you in some way."[12] By way of example, he described the moment when Becky, one of many Scottish immigrants who had come to Nauvoo as a result of a proselytizing campaign launched in the United Kingdom by Smith and his associates, begs to be baptized right away: "But I've had a feelin'. And it's not a feelin' I conjured up m'self. I can't explain it, but I know it's true!"[13] "Now who would ever say such a thing?" Warner laughed, "but someone did and when you put it up on the stage, you think there's something really fresh and wonderful about that. It's always unbelievable to imagine how truth really is."[14] To fashion the most honest and accurate script he could, Warner recruited a team of eight LDS members—writers, historians, academics, homemakers—whose only commonality was "a desire to speak to this audience."[15] He commissioned the pageant music in a similar manner, enlisting seven composers from across the country to procure period music and to integrate it into a newly fashioned musical score, which, in the style of nineteenth-century melodrama, underscores the entire show to suggest mood and heighten emotion. Warner emphasized that the entire writing team was unpaid and that all signed away their rights to the work and gave them to the LDS as part of their service commitment to the Church.[16]

The idea of "re-membering" was equally important to the acting company, who emphasized that in order to portray these characters, they have to be "living like and with the same faith as the people we are telling the story about."[17] Dallyn Bayles, the Equity actor and devout Mormon who plays the role of Joseph Smith, explained his approach by quoting the critical line that both opens and closes the play: "When you're here, we're here." "There's a connection with the people who came before and where we are now," Bayles said. "We are who we are and that's what we bring to the stage. We're telling the story of these people who lived 150 years ago, but we are doing so honestly, living and working together in a very Christ-like, kind, loving, family-oriented community which emulates their experience."[18] This perspective was particularly helpful for the nonprofessional family cast members—150 men, women, and children who provide the onstage crowds that literally build the town (we watch foundations being dug and scenographic buildings being erected) over the course of the show—who were faced with what initially looked like a daunting acting challenge. "My wife and I were trying to figure out how we should be acting and what we should be doing and who we should be representing," one amateur actor explained. "As we performed and finally started to understand, we realized that we were just supposed to be us. We're in love and we care for each other and we care for our family and that is what we represented on stage."[19]

Since the performing arts are an LDS-sanctioned part of their religious life, church members are eager to partake in the pageants in the manner most appropriate to their talents. Recruitment doesn't seem to be an issue; in fact, performers engage in arduous auditions for the "core cast" roles, which are mostly filled by highly trained actors, singers, and dancers who receive minimal compensation for their work (one actor told me that his check covered only about one-eighth of expenses for him, his wife, and five children, all of whom were performing). Thousands of LDS members apply online to be accepted into one of the five 150-member family casts engaged for the five-week summer run of the pageant. Each cast spends two weeks in Nauvoo; the first week is devoted to daytime rehearsals with the core cast and nightly observations of performances. They also serve as the principal performers in the extensive preshow, which involves audience members in an interactive experience of nineteenth-century life in Nauvoo that includes log sawing, branding, quilting, handcart pulls, tugs-of-war, relay and sack races, children's games and crafts, and round dancing. During the second week, that group performs in the pageant while the next family cast rehearses and assumes the preshow duties. The families that come "save up during the year" and treat the experience as their summer vacation. Not only are they not compensated, but they aren't even identified, which is also true of everyone else involved in the show. There is absolutely no playbill or other acknowledgment of any kind. When I mentioned the difficulties of this for a historian writing about their work, they all laughed sympathetically but told me unequivocally that "we wouldn't be comfortable with that [a playbill] because we are doing this for the glory of God."[20] This is a second critical parallel between Mormon pageants and medieval Christian art and theatre practices, a discourse to be explored in another paper.

Company members are well aware of the long-honored position the performing arts enjoy in the life of their church and frequently quote the official sanctions that justify their involvement. The oft-repeated quote from the Book of Mormon, the first of three sanctioned texts espousing LDS theology, is viewed as the foundational blessing for artistic endeavors: "Men are that they might have joy" (2 Nephi 2:22–25). As soon as Nauvoo became an established town, Smith was quick to introduce elements of joyful celebration of God via various choral, instrumental, and dramatic organizations and the all-night dance parties that he hosted. Young was even more effusive in his love of the arts, for as early as 1834 he was quoted as saying, "If I were placed on a cannibal island and given a task of civilizing its people, I should straightway build a theatre."[21] When, in 1844, Thomas A. Lyne, a tragic actor from Philadelphia who was brought to Nauvoo by Smith to mount productions for the new Nauvoo Dramatic Society housed in the Cultural Hall, cast Young in the role of the Peruvian high priest in his production of *Pizarro, or the Death of Rolla,* advertised as a "grand moral entertainment," Young's devotion was cemented. Several years later, after the Mormons arrived in the Salt Lake Valley, Young commissioned first a temple and, one day later, a public building to house theatrical productions and other cultural activities; by 1861 he had built a mammoth, well-appointed theatre that rivaled similar venues throughout the country and became a popular touring house that attracted major performers of the period. Back in Nauvoo and even during the thirteen-hundred-mile westward migration, Young avidly endorsed not only theatrical entertainments but music and dance as well. Two nights before the first group of Mormons began the exodus in February 1846, the Nauvoo Brass Band noted the following in their recorded minutes:

> February 9. By request of Brother B. Young, the band met in the upper room of the Temple, played a few tunes, after which Brother Young arose and said that, as we were about to leave Nauvoo, we had come together, to pass off the evening, and that he thought it no harm to have a little recreation in singing, etc., as long as it was done in righteousness. He then called on the Lord to take charge of the meeting; the brethren and sisters then joined in and danced.[22]

Young affirmed his commitment on January 14, 1847, from his Winter Quarters on the trek west as "the will of the Lord" by proclaiming "if thou art merry, praise the Lord with singing, with music, with dancing," which became part of the sacred *Doctrines & Covenants,* section 136, verse 28.[23]

Hence, it was easy for Warner to justify the textual and production choices of telling the Nauvoo story through theatre, music, and dance. The creative team of eight book writers and seven composers could legitimately exercise artistic license in their choice of material, since historically the Mormons were known for their eclecticism. Their music, for instance, was described by some period observers as an "odd mix of sensibilities" that collapsed "the sacred into the mundane and vice versa" and resulted in musical programs "blending the sacred, sentimental, and comic."[24] The historian Terryl Givens asserts that it was "during the Nauvoo era that music would increasingly be associated in Mormon culture with recreation and entertainment," which he found "emblematic of one of Mormonism's most distinctive developments. . . . In the sphere of music, as in most every other realm," Givens states, "Mormonism's absence of an ecclesiastical line of demarcation between the sacred and the secular would prove to be as typical of the new faith as it was idiosyncratic in American religious culture."[25]

Warner and company capture this sensibility perfectly in the nonstop action of the pageant, which moves seamlessly from worship to labor, to mundane chores of everyday life, to unabashed celebration. As the narrator character, Parley Pratt, says near the beginning of the pageant, "As the music of life fills our souls, we rejoice."[26] A good example is this tightly compressed scene, which lasts no more than a few minutes. A character announces, "In coming together to build a temple, we also came together to celebrate the wonders and beauties of life and to express them in the most graceful ways of music, of drama, and dancing"; another proclaims, "The Nauvoo Dramatic Society announces its opening performance of the tragedy *Pizarro* to be staged here in the Cultural Hall featuring as an Incan Priest our very own Brigham Young." Whoops and shouts follow: "C'mon everyone, let's dance." Round dancing segues into Scottish bagpipes and folk dance, which morphs into Broadway-style song and dance. Immediately thereafter the characters join in collective prayer and hymn singing.[27]

The pageant also celebrates the unrelenting spirit of optimism that, no doubt, is largely responsible for the Mormons' survival and growth as a religious community. This is reflected in the careful choice of which historical incidents are dramatized and which are relegated to narration. The "spirit of buoyancy" that "infuses Mormon expectations and finds expression in Mormon art," according to one LDS critic, deemphasizes or even eliminates elements of "misery, degradation, and hopelessness" in the historical narrative.[28] It would be misleading, however, to relate Nauvoo's history without discussing Smith's almost constant harassments and legal entanglements, as well as his murder by an unruly mob while he awaited trial in the Carthage, Illinois, jail. The fact that the community continued to be under siege even after Smith's death is equally important; otherwise, why did the group embark on the mass exodus west? Warner made sure this information was included but handled deftly so as to maintain the all-important spirit of optimism. The decision to eliminate the most stageworthy scenes, however, couldn't have been easy for a professionally trained theatre director and PhD historian, who obviously understands the power of theatricality. Warner discussed his natural predilection toward creating a classic protagonist/antagonist tale and his eventual decision, under the guidance of church leaders, to avoid that approach. "It's easy for us to represent ourselves as martyrs, as the beleaguered and the persecuted," he said, "but we didn't want to do that here; we want our story to be hopeful."[29] This position gained added importance once he realized that many members of the local audience were descendants of Smith's persecutors and murderers. Hence, the facts of "misery, degradation, and hopelessness" that must be told are relegated to narrators who use them as transitional material to move the story forward chronologically. The narrators also link one major staged event to the next as collective enactments of endearing tales from letters and diaries that all demonstrate Smith's power as prophet, church leader, and community builder. Those historical details that do not enhance Smith's stature, particularly those surrounding his pronouncements on polygamy and the multifarious problems provoked by his own multiple marriages, are never mentioned in the pageant.[30] These, as well as his numerous other arrests, are absent, alluded to vaguely, or simply dismissed as "false charges."[31] In Warner's defense, however, it would be unusual for the text of any historical pageant to include information denigrating the play's hero, particularly when the larger intent is to commemorate his birth, life, and importance to civic and religious history.

Confronted with the challenge of creating a powerful pageant and needing, for various reasons, to avoid the most inherently dramatic historical events, Warner wisely turned to the fact that Smith had commanded the erection of a prosperous city in a mosquito-infested swamp in less than three years' time. That the LDS was in the process of reconstructing the greatest of Smith's creations, the visually stunning temple on the hill overlooking the city and the Mississippi River beyond, was an added incentive to use it as the centerpiece, literally and figuratively, of the play. The first thing they did was to relocate the theatre, which for the previous pageant had been in a different part of town, so that the actual temple would become the theatrical backdrop. They then ensured that the major action of the play would be the building of the temple, a project that conveniently extended beyond Smith's murder so that the pageant ends not in death but with the hope of the future. The main narrator, Parley Pratt, says:

> And so we walked down Parley Street, and we crossed the Mississippi and with one last glance back at our beloved temple, we turned our wagons west. Over the years, time and the forces of nature erased almost all the work we had done here with such love and desire. One by one, the temple

> stones were scattered throughout these parts. And for decades, the foundation was plowed over and used as a field. Nothing, nothing could erase what Nauvoo had given us. That we took with us and we taught our children and they taught their children, which is why, when you're here, we're here also.[32]

As he delivers this speech the audience is looking at the scenographically constructed wood-frame, two-story temple with a cupola on top, which has been built and raised, similarly to an old-fashioned barn-raising, on the stage over the course of the play. This activity happily engaged the entire 150-strong family cast at one time or another: the men doing the heavy construction work, the women creating the fabric walls, the children serving as gofers and general helpers. Now, as Pratt describes how the temple fell into ruin, the stage set is razed; it goes down as one massive piece off the raked upstage edge of the show deck. Characters return to the stage to chitchat and, once again, recognize the audience as friends and soul mates: "We know you and you know us," the actor playing Pratt's wife says. This interlude not only directly engages the audience but also heightens the tension as the narrative moves toward its climactic moment. It is now pitch-black outside, and the only lighting is provided by stage instruments. The stage has also dimmed to black so that a monologue can be delivered simultaneous to the gradual illumination of the real temple, with the golden figure of the Angel Moroni on top:

> Today, facing west on the high bluffs overlooking the city of Nauvoo thence across the Mississippi, and over the plains of Iowa, there stands Joseph's temple, a magnificent house of God. Here in the Salt Lake Valley, facing east to that beautiful temple in Nauvoo, stands Brigham's temple, the Salt Lake Temple. They look towards one another as bookends between which there are volumes that speak of the thousands who made the long journey from the Mississippi River.[33]

By the end of the speech, the temple is positively gleaming against the night sky, and the full company, backed by a taped recording of the Mormon Tabernacle Choir, is singing a rousing hymn. Just to prolong the dramatic moment, and underscore the religious implications of the scene, there is doctrinal dialogue and then an even more stirring crescendo and final flourish from the choir. The older gentleman sitting next to me promptly burst into tears and joined the thunderous applause surrounding us. The cast, maintaining its sense of humility and honor to God, did one company bow and then invited the audience to come say hello before they left. For whatever meaning this spectacle held for the many LDS members in the audience, for this nonbeliever it was, at the very least, stunning theatricality.

Those audience members requiring more detailed history and biography can attend any of six vignettes performed during daylight hours and in appropriate settings throughout the town, many of which are truly "hallowed ground." *Go Ye into the World*, in which historic church elders discuss their missionary experiences abroad, is performed in the Seventies Hall, which was used in the 1840s for just such lectures, instruction, and testimonials. Intimate marital details of Smith and his wife are excerpted from correspondence and performed as *Letters of Joseph & Emma* across the street from their actual home, Mansion House, which is referenced in the play.[34] The most historically and dramatically effective vignette, "The Trail of Hope," allows the audience to actually walk the migratory footpath of the 1846–47 exodus, stopping at different performance stations to listen to characters, poised in front of informational historical markers quoting their recorded words, relate tales of the fear, uncertainty, and hardship entailed in leaving Nauvoo. The actor portraying Bathsheba Smith quotes her diary to describe the experience of "making the beds, sweeping out the house, tidying up, and then closing the door, never to return."[35] The play is presented in the early morning, emulating the time when the refugees would have set out on their journey west. This performance once again borrows historic precedent from the medieval theatre practice of having the audience travel from one play to the next while the performers remain stationary, awaiting the arrival of the next group before repeating the play. There are also parallels to the Christian practice of the devout walking the Stations of the Cross, which depict in pictures, words, or tableaux the Passion of Christ. Each station or marker signifies a major event in the final week of his life on Earth, from his condemnation to death to his being laid in the tomb, and is accompanied by special prayers and meditation. For the Mormons, leaving Nauvoo was a symbolic death only to be followed by a rebirth, through the risen Christ, in the promised land of the Utah territory, and the vignette is designed for contemporary audiences to pause and reflect on that heritage. The physical experience of walking the trail in the early morning sun as it leads to the Mississippi River is itself high drama; the twelve performances that breathe life into the historical markers along the way serve to underscore that "you are here on the hallowed ground where these historic people lived," ultimately making the performances powerful. As Barbara Kirshenblatt-Gimblett has said, "The actual spot" of history "is remarkably mute"; it is present-day actors who allow the voices of history to be heard.[36]

Although this essay profiles only the Nauvoo pageant, all seven pageants share the basic approach and components discussed here, if on a less sophisticated level. The work at Nauvoo is expected to become the model, however, for reconceiving existing pageants and creating new ones and for good reason. The Mormons have found an effective means of commemorating and promoting their heritage, as well as religio-cultural tourism, via their deft combination of the various forms of pageants with outdoor historical drama. This construction supports some of their most cherished values: the building and sustaining of community through a collective, performative experience; the creation of enormous theatres that feature large-scale scenery, lighting, and spectacle to further enhance the power of their message (particularly the religious elements) and bring together thousands of spectator-participants; the mellifluous incorporation of and emphasis on drama, dance, and music in the crafting of their story; the inclusion of parades, processions, and other ceremonial elements appropriate to outdoor pageantry; an emphasis on being outdoors and the importance of the natural and constructed environments (both the Mississippi River and the Nauvoo temple are equally important components of the Nauvoo pageant) in the narrative; and the realization of an eternal present—"when you're here, we're here"—in dramatizing the historic past. As Paul Connerton points out, commemorative ceremonies provide dramatic means of encountering past events in the present, allowing communities to understand their "past as a kind of collective autobiography."[37]

Finally, and perhaps most important, the Mormon pageants effectively offer alternative narratives of the forging of the American nation. Although the unalloyed cheeriness and exuberance of the characters, even in the face of sorrow and defeat, can be grating to nonpartisan audiences, they relate tales of successful endurance and prosperity that resulted in the establishment of a thriving, extremely wealthy, religion that boasts thirteen million members worldwide. Clearly the pageants relate a simplified and sanitized version of history, but all historical dramas are shaped to provide uplifting messages and positive portrayals of complex situations and characters such as Joseph Smith. LDS members, particularly those with formal training in performing arts, are arguably the best choice to shape and perform these "symphonic dramas of American history," since their ancestors built not just cities but a major American religion.

Notes

1. Paul Green, *The Lost Colony: A Symphonic Drama of American History,* ed. Laurence G. Avery (Chapel Hill: University of North Carolina Press, 1954).

2. Scott J. Parker, former director of the Institute for Outdoor Drama, interview by author, tape recording, Chapel Hill, NC, July 18, 2005.

3. Leonard J. Arrington and Davis Bitton, *The Mormon Experience* (New York: Alfred A. Knopf, 1979), 62.

4. Edwin Brown Firmage and Richard Collin Mangrum, *Zion in the Courts: A Legal History of the Church of Jesus Christ of Latter-Day Saints, 1830–1900* (Urbana: University of Illinois Press, 1988), 61; also see E. E. Ericksen, *The Psychological and Ethical Aspects of Mormon Group Life* (Salt Lake City: University of Utah Press, 1922).

5. Sarah Barringer Gordon, *The Mormon Question: Polygamy and Constitutional Conflict in Nineteenth Century America* (Chapel Hill: University of North Carolina Press, 2002), 56.

6. Arrington and Bitton, *The Mormon Experience,* 46–57.

7. Gordon, *The Mormon Question,* 55–57.

8. Rodney Stark, *The Rise of Mormonism,* ed. Reid L. Neilson (New York: Columbia University Press, 2005), 29.

9. David Glassberg, *American Historical Pageantry* (Chapel Hill: University of North Carolina Press, 1990), 4.

10. Douglas J. Davies, *An Introduction to Mormonism* (Cambridge, UK: Cambridge University Press, 2003), 28–29.

11. Unidentified audience member, Nauvoo Pageant Talk-Back, taped by the author, Aug. 2, 2007.

12. David T. Warner, interview by the author, Temple Square in Salt Lake City, Aug. 8, 2007.

13. Nauvoo Pageant, transcript of performance, taped by the author, Aug. 2, 2007.

14. Warner interview.

15. Ibid.

16. Ibid.

17. Gayle Lockwood, pageant musical director, Nauvoo Pageant Talk-Back, taped by the author, Aug. 2, 2007.

18. Dallyn Bayles, pageant actor, Nauvoo Pageant Talk-Back, taped by the author, Aug. 2, 2007.

19. Family cast member, audience participant, Nauvoo Pageant Talk-Back, taped by the author, Aug. 2, 2007.

20. Anonymous actors, Nauvoo Pageant Talk-Back, taped by the author, Aug. 1, 2007.

21. Terryl L. Givens, *People of Paradox: A History of Mormon Culture* (Oxford: Oxford University Press, 2007), 146.

22. *Contributor* 1, no. 9 (June 1880): 197; cited in Givens, *People of Paradox,* 130.

23. Givens, *People of Paradox,* 135.

24. Michael Hicks, *Mormonism and Music: A History* (Urbana: University of Illinois Press, 1989), 60; cited in Givens, *People of Paradox,* 134.

25. Givens, *People of Paradox,* 127.

26. Pageant transcript, 1.

27. Ibid., 4.

28. Lorin F. Wheelwright, ed., *Mormon Arts: Volume One* (Provo, Utah: Brigham Young University Press, 1972), 2; cited in Givens, *People of Paradox,* 152.

29. Warner interview.

30. For more information on the life and work of Joseph Smith see Fawn Brodie, *No Man Knows My History: The Life of Joseph Smith, the Mormon Prophet* (New York: Alfred A. Knopf, 1945); Richard Lyman Bushman, *Joseph Smith and the Beginnings of Mormonism* (Urbana: University of Illinois Press, 1984); Richard Lyman Bushman, *Joseph Smith: Rough Stone Rolling* (New York: Alfred A. Knopf, 2005).

31. Pageant transcript, 5.

32. Ibid., 6.

33. Ibid., 7.

34. The historic building could not be used for the performance, presumably because it is owned and maintained by a rival faction of the LDS, the Community of Christ (previously the Reorganized Church of Jesus Christ of Latter-Day Saints), which formed shortly after Smith's death, with his son Joseph Smith III as its leader and with headquarters in Independence, Missouri. Interestingly, the Community of Christ owns some of the more historically significant sites in Nauvoo, including Joseph Smith's original homestead, his Red Brick Store, which provided his livelihood as he built both town and religion, and the Smith family cemetery, and charges a nominal fee for the walking tour of its properties. Although the Community does not offer live performances, the instructional film and information in its separate visitor's center provides a fascinating perspective on the complex development of Mormonism after Smith's death.

35. "Trail of Hope," vignette transcript, 2.

36. Barbara Kirshenblatt-Gimblett, *Destination Culture* (Berkeley: University of California Press, 1998), 9.

37. Paul Connerton, *How Societies Remember* (Cambridge, UK: Cambridge University Press, 1989), 70.

"Look at the Moon"

Hunter Hills Theatre; Outdoor Drama in the Smokies

Charlotte Headrick and Andrew Vorder Bruegge

We spent our summers
Singing dancing growing up
Emoting romancing living hard
Spilling our guts dropping our guard
Shaking our butts underneath the stars
Boys and girls together
A little faster in stormy weather

—Jon Lutz, "We Spent Our Summers: An Elegy to Hunter Hills Theatre," unpublished poem, 1986.

THE POEM "We Spent Our Summers: An Elegy to Hunter Hills Theatre," by Jon Lutz, captures something of what it was like to be a part of the remarkable experience that was Hunter Hills Theatre. This summer program left a lasting legacy in the annals of outdoor drama because it was unique. Many colleges have operated summer theatre programs, but few have had a program of the scope, artistic vision, or operational format of Hunter Hills Theatre. It was a fabulous showcase for the talent of the University of Tennessee theatre program. It was also a very ambitious and complicated program to run.

This essay traces the development of the theatre, its place in the history of the University of Tennessee theatre program, and its place in outdoor drama. For seven summers during the twelve years of the theatre's existence, Charlotte Headrick and Andrew Vorder Bruegge were members of the company.

Hunter Hills Theatre was built in 1955 for *Chucky Jack,* an outdoor drama about the first governor of Tennessee, John Sevier, who was portrayed in 1957 by John Cullum, a Knoxville native. The Maples family of Gatlinburg had built the theatre hoping to keep tourists on the west side of the Smokies rather than having them go over the mountains to Cherokee, North Carolina, to see *Unto These Hills.* The outdoor drama limped along for a few years and in 1959 finally closed. Several factors caused its demise. According to Bill Morgan, who worked in the University of Tennessee Development Office during the Hunter Hills Theatre years, the play opened to mixed reviews and at nearly three hours long was simply too long, but Kermit Hunter refused to cut a word.[1] *Chucky Jack* may not have been successful because the story of the show was not strongly linked to "hallowed ground." At the 2008 Theatre Symposium, Mark R. Sumner, director emeritus of the Institute of Outdoor Drama (IOD), made a convincing argument about the essential link between success of an outdoor drama and its association with "hallowed ground." Examples of this concept are the two outdoor historic dramas at Snow Camp, North Carolina, *Sword of Peace* and *Pathway to Freedom.* Snow Camp is one of the historic Quaker settlements in North Carolina, and the location of the theatre is in the heart of the settlement. That land is in a real sense "hallowed." Moreover, the historical story of John Sevier certainly was not as well-known to tourists as tales surrounding mythical figures like Daniel Boone or the melodramatic story of the Trail of Tears, for example. Tourists came to Gatlinburg to see the Smoky Mountains in a generic way, without any specific historical motivation. Also, *Chucky Jack* lacked the surefire religious appeal of *The Book of Job* in Kentucky or one of the Passion plays.

After *Chucky Jack* ceased operations, the space was used as a rental venue for music events—one summer the Washington Ballet used the facility, and Union College performed there another summer. It was dark a couple of seasons, and then the Maples family gave the theatre to the University of Tennessee as a tax write-off. In December of 1965 Dr. Edward Boling, vice president of Development for the University of Tennessee, announced the gift of Hunter Hills Theatre to the university by Mr. and Mrs. R. L. Maples. The gift was valued at $300,000.

In 1966 the Department of Speech and Theatre mounted the first productions. From 1966 to 1977 the University of Tennessee produced a variety of plays, from musicals such as *The Sound of Music, Oklahoma!, South Pacific,* and *Annie Get Your Gun,* to plays such as *Everyman, Dark of the Moon,* and *Indians,* to Shakespeare's *A Midsummer Night's Dream,* and a legendary, one-night stand of Aeschylus's *Agamemnon.*[2] The productions of well-known Broadway musicals were intended to appeal to the broad population of tourists. The Smoky Mountains National Park has long been the most visited National Park in the United States, so the artistic director of Hunter Hills Theatre, Fred Fields, was counting on sheer volume of potential audience to carry the operation along to financial success. Furthermore, the opportunities for night life in the Gatlinburg area were very limited at that time, for the town offered only a few small venues for dancing, bluegrass music, children's entertainment, and one licensed tavern. The theatre offered a family-oriented evening of entertainment to a vast audience of tourists looking for something to do after a day of exploring the Smokies or strolling along the streets of Gatlinburg. The theatre was also intended to appeal to supporters of the university who lived in the region.

Most years, Hunter Hills Theatre operated with a rolling repertory season with performances Tuesday through Sunday, and the repertory plot called for each show to run at least twice per week. Typically, a season included two musicals and *Dark of the Moon*. Along with the artistic director's decision to anchor each summer season with major Broadway musicals, the rolling repertory format was intended to capture the maximum attendance from tourists who visited the area for several days to a week. With the rolling repertory format the theatre could turn patrons into "repeat customers" by offering a variety of productions during any tourists' stay in the Smokies. If they liked *Oklahoma!*, for example, then they might come back the next night to see *Dark of the Moon*. Ticket prices were modest. Five dollars purchased a general admission, and there was ample parking on the theatre property. The University of Tennessee staged thirty-two productions using more than five hundred actors and technicians (most of whom were UT students) during its twelve years of operating Hunter Hills Theatre. Fred Fields was managing director for eleven of those twelve years. He was assisted by many artists and artistic organizations during his tenure—choreographers, music directors, costume and scenic designers. The theatre played to many thousands of tourists over the years.

The facility was perfectly situated in an isolated setting on the fringes of the Great Smoky Mountains National Park, with the audience facing a wonderful vista of Mount LeConte out over the stage. Very little ambient light or sound intruded into the space (compared to facilities such as the Harrodsburg, Kentucky, downtown setting for *The Legend of Daniel Boone*). A buffer of trees surrounded the facility on three sides, and the sawdust stage complemented the setting of many of the productions.

The theatre offered three vertical playing levels (stage, blockhouse, and upper stage) plus a grassy "pit" situated between the audience and the stage that could serve as a possible fourth level. (The productions of *A Midsummer Night's Dream* and *Agamemnon* did use this fourth playing level, for example.) The theatre also featured three horizontal playing areas across the main stage level—the center stage and two turntables left and right. This provided no less than five playing areas at any one time. The two turntables created two or more additional playing areas as needed. Turntables were a popular form of stage machinery in the 1950s. They offered a theatrical flair to productions (e.g., *Hello, Dolly*), but, more important, they made the staging of multiple productions in a repertory schedule easier to manage *(Oklahoma!* in combination with *The Sound of Music* and *Dark of the Moon).*

The amphitheatre seated about sixteen hundred theatregoers—a smaller venue than several of the other Sumner/Hunter summer theatres. The rake of the amphitheatre was very low, compared to other outdoor facilities such as *Unto These Hills* or the *Black Hills Passion Play,* and this presented some acoustical challenges. To compensate, an improvised system of sound amplification and monitors was rigged for the three main playing areas and for the orchestra. The original design of the theatre included two light towers situated on the far left and right sides of the amphitheatre, about two-thirds of the way up the slope. There were wing positions for instruments situated backstage left and right. Two much larger light towers were added in the early 1970s, centered in the amphitheatre. The positioning of these towers, combined with more modern lighting instruments and circuitry, greatly improved the quality of lighting for the productions. These towers did cut off about five hundred seats in the uppermost section of the amphitheatre, seats that were rarely filled during the ten years of performances in the 1960s and 1970s. The loss of these empty seats was more than compensated for by the improved lighting capabilities.

The artistic director assembled his staff and student company primarily from the UT theatre program. This created a cohesion and stability in personnel and artistic vision. Hardly any other outdoor theatre operation has ever used this model. The staff included the artistic director, one costume designer/costumier, one lighting/sound designer, one technical director, one food service manager (reassigned from the university's on-campus food service), one box office/publicity manager, one music director/conductor, one choreographer, and a resident facilities manager employed through the university's Physical Plant office on a twelve-month contract. In some years the artistic staff included one scenic designer and a company manager. Many of these artistic staff positions provided valuable experience for graduate students or recent graduates of the program. The company of performers typically included twenty to twenty-five students, two or three paid professional performers in principal roles, two or three local high school students to handle landscaping and concessions, two cooks, and two or three professional musicians.

The artistic director cast the company during the spring on the university campus in Knoxville. Rehearsal began immediately thereafter and continued through early June on campus. This meant that most of the rehearsal and some production work was completed prior to the summer. The operations moved to Gatlinburg at the conclusion of the spring quarter in early June. The company quickly built the shows and conducted dress rehearsals through mid-June. By the last week of June all the productions for the summer had opened, and the season ran until late August or even Labor Day.

The operation provided all needs to the company—housing, food, wages—so that everyone could focus on the artistic agenda. From 1967 through 1974 all company members received room and board in the Gatlinburg-Pittman High School, conveniently located just beyond the theatre's parking lot. The company used the school's locker rooms for showers; the kitchen and cafeteria provided space to prepare and serve four meals per day. Occasionally, a singer or two was hired to perform and did no other work. No students were paid for their performances, but student company members were paid between $1.25 and $1.65 per hour to work during the day on activities such as building scenery and making costumes, conducting publicity activities and serving on box-office shifts, laundering and maintaining wardrobe, rotating sets, and cleaning the theatre facility. Students could earn up to six hours of university credit most years. The facility included storage space for costume stock, scenery stock, company bed frames, mattresses, and wardrobes. Hunter Hills Theatre enjoyed access to a variety of the university's resources. This included at least two vehicles, access to the Department of Speech and Theatre's scenic and costume stock and studios, recycled construction materials, tools, bedding, and furniture.

Considering the burgeoning operation that involved rental of housing facilities and the expense of providing board for a large company, it was not surprising that the production budget remained lean over the years. Costumes received the bulk of the production budget, for that element provided the most exciting spectacle onstage. Scenery was sparse but monumental and versatile. Scenic units were reworked and used in many shows over the years. Season selection also played a role in stretching the production budget. Since *Dark of the Moon* was produced nearly every year, for example, there was a stock of costumes and scenery that stood ever ready to support that show. Musicals such as *Hello, Dolly* or *Oklahoma!* typically ran for two years in order to get a return on the substantial investment in their costumes and scenery.

Although each season would be dominated by productions of large, popular musicals, the artistic director, Fred Fields, made Howard Richardson and Richard Berney's *Dark of the Moon* the "signature" show of Hunter Hills Theatre. Starting in 1967, it was produced every year including a one-night stand of the play in 1973, performed especially to honor Fields when the show was not included in the regular repertory of productions. Written in 1942 at the University of Iowa, *Dark of the Moon* dramatizes the traditional ballad of Barbara Allen, weaving the ballad with legends of mountain witches, folk drama, and the local color of the Appalachian setting. John, the Witch Boy, has become enamored of the sensual Barbara Allen. Through a spell cast by the Conjur Woman he is transformed into a human. He will remain human as long as Barbara is true to him for a year. If she is not, he will revert back to a witch, and her death is the price of her unfaithfulness. As a witch he will live three hundred years, and then he will become fog on the mountain.

Dark of the Moon has received mixed reviews as a play since its first production in Iowa. Over the years numerous community theatres, high schools, and colleges have produced the piece. In some cases there has been community outrage that a local school was producing a play about witches. There are scenes, characters, and situations in the drama that appear hackneyed, melodramatic, and stereotyped, perhaps giving credence to the legend that Richardson and Berney wrote the play as satire. Fields's vision of the play, in the magnificent setting at Hunter Hills Theatre, was on the opposite end of the dramatic spectrum from satire and eschewed lowbrow interpretation. For example, Fields set the action at an inexact time in the distant, misty past that gave the production a feeling of folk myth. Where the original text refers to a "social worker," the line became "school marm." Fields also deleted the embarrassingly stereotypical dialogue about moonshine. Most significant, he incorporated much traditional and sacred music into the play, an addition that greatly enriched the drama. The Hunter Hills Theatre version of the script began and ended with "Down in the Valley," and the other music ranged from a rollicking "Wildwood Flower," "One Morning in May" (accompanied by a country folk dance), to the melancholy "Lesson Too Late for the Learning," to the cluster of hymns in the emotionally driven revival scene: "Golden Bells," "Just As I Am," "No, Never Alone," "Rock of Ages," and others. To this day, put a group of cast members together, and we can drop into four-part harmony with these songs. With the magnificence of the Smokies surrounding the theatre, with the authentic sound of Appalachia in most actors' ears, with melodies of traditional sacred music harmoniously flowing from the actors' mouths, and with Scots-Irish ancestry running in the blood of many of the actors, there was a sense of respect and wonder in the cast. If anyone had ever tried to portray a character ironically or satirically, Fred Fields would have stopped that interpretation.

One cannot imagine a more perfect environment for a production of *Dark of the Moon* than Hunter Hills Theatre. Those most ancient of mountains, the Smokies, were in actuality the backdrop for the play. On the nights when the real moon came out from behind the clouds in the final, climactic scene on top of the mountain, the effect seemed indeed miraculous. When these theatrical and natural phenomena converged as if on cue, audible gasps were heard from audience members. The title of this essay is taken from the final moment of *Dark of the Moon,* when John the Witch Boy stands over the dead body of his wife, Barbara Allen. After living as a human with her for a year, he is now transformed back to a witch. During his time as a human, John had not been able to see the moon because of the spell cast on him by the Conjur Woman. Now a witch again, his final words of the play are "Look at the moon!"[3]

If any play came near to capturing Sumner's idea of "hallowed ground," it was *Dark of the Moon.* But unlike the usual template for outdoor dramas that deal with historical characters and are site specific, *Dark of the Moon* was not written for Hunter Hills Theatre and did not deal with any historical characters. The Appalachian setting of the play in the real mountains that the play refers to made the Hunter Hills annual production of *Dark of the Moon* sacred and hallowed. This signature piece, shaped so earnestly by Fields, was much closer to the Appalachian spirit than *Chucky Jack* could ever be.

Mildred Dunnock, the original Linda Loman in the Broadway production of *Death of a Salesman,* was a guest at the Tennessee Theatre Association convention in Gatlinburg in 1969. Fields asked the Hunter Hills Theatre cast to return on a September night following the season to present a special performance of *Dark of the Moon* for Ms. Dunnock and the convention attendees. Afterward, Dunnock spoke to the cast about what a special evening it had been for her and the rest of the audience. Her praise confirmed what we already knew. Many of us have experienced theatre magic in various forms, but the blend of the natural beauty of the setting, all that talent, coupled with that play and Fields's vision for it, expanded with music and dance, was hard to top. For some of us it is still a benchmark of excellence.

Fred Fields provided overarching artistic and executive leadership to the Hunter Hills Theatre venture, and he guided all aspects of the operation to attain that benchmark level of excellence. The opportunity to work in rolling repertory format was invaluable for the students. It was not unusual to have four plays in one's head, and few undergraduates have ever had this kind of training and the experience of running a play for thirty or more performances. Moreover, virtually all the productions were directed by Fields, and his directorial vision provided an artistic unity to the productions. Rehearsing the productions on campus in a large classroom, he could visualize a plan to transform each theatrical moment to the various playing areas of the Hunter Hills space—main stage, grassy field in front of the stage, two side stages on turntables (four-scene setup), and two raised stages. He also used entrances from the woods surrounding the theatre, especially the stage-right area. Throughout the rehearsal process Fields gave very few notes, but one learned to listen to the notes he gave to others, which really would inform any performance. Lorraine Dowell, a longtime costumer, referred to him as the "kid glove director." His gentle style worked well for guiding young performers. He had an uncanny ability to cast well, and he created beautiful stage pictures, using the stage, the actors, movement, music, and, of course, the Smokies to tell the story. A former air force officer, Fields maintained an aura of the military about him that inspired loyalty to his values, respect for his expertise, and confidence in his vision.

While Fred Fields achieved success with his artistic vision and educational mission at Hunter Hills Theatre, he was less successful at making the operation a popular, successful entertainment venue in Gatlinburg. It never attained attendance levels or local support to match its competitor on the other side of the mountains in Cherokee, North Carolina. Attendance at Hunter Hills Theatre peaked at about twelve hundred per night for *The Sound of Music* in 1971. For other productions, houses usually were between four and six hundred on any given night. The theatre's disappointing track record over the years might be explained at least in part by the cool relationship between the theatre and the local Gatlinburg business community. Pat Conroy, in his *Prince of Tides,* describes the difference between mountain people and island people: "mountaineers are isolates; islanders are citizens of the world. An islander greets the stranger with a wave; a mountaineer wonders why he came."[4]

Bill Morgan asserts that the relationship between *Chucky Jack* and the community of Gatlinburg was not strong in the 1950s, and Gatlinburg natives—the old timers—had always been suspicious of the university. Morgan believes that the skepticism generated among Gatlinburg natives by the *Chucky Jack* experience also tainted their attitudes toward the university's venture a decade later. He believes that the lack of wholehearted local support from the very beginning contributed significantly to the ultimate demise of the university's program. Without the direct, active, enthusiastic support of the local business community, the theatre never was able to generate revenue at a level that could justify its long-term survival to university administrators. A former dean of the College of Liberal Arts (later the College of Arts and Sciences), Lorayne Lester, recounts that "Hunter Hills was funded directly from the Chancellor's Office, so no one in the Department knew much about their finances. . . . All the department did was pay Fred a summer stipend."[5]

While the chancellor and other university leaders generously sustained the Hunter Hills Theatre operation for more than a decade, they eventually had to direct always-finite resources elsewhere. In a recent message Tom Cooke, former chair of the theatre program at the University of Tennessee and artistic director of Hunter Hills Theatre for its final season, reflects on the theatre's financial weaknesses:

> No one knows all of the many considerations that went into the decision to close Hunter Hills or who made those decisions. The company of [1977] knew the fate of the theatre had been decided and that we were just doing one more summer to meet obligations the university had made. . . . The rains came, and came, and, in spite of the best efforts of . . . a fantastic company, we lost money and probably confirmed feelings that the theatre would always be a financial drain. There had been complaints for years and I guess cost will always be the bottom line with administrators. But I believe it would have been difficult for them to close it if Fred [Fields] had remained healthy. His tenacity had seen the theatre through some very difficult times.[6]

Indeed, Fred Fields had committed himself passionately to the success of Hunter Hills Theatre for more than a decade. He was Hunter Hills Theatre. When he was no longer able to direct the theatre after 1976, no one remained to speak out on behalf of the theatre to administrators or to the Gatlinburg community. In Knoxville the new chair of the theatre, Ralph Allen, had ambitious goals for the theatre program that were focused on the Clarence Brown Professional Company. Without support from the Gatlinburg community or university support at the department or administrative level, Hunter Hills Theatre was destined to close. Bill Morgan writes of the closing:

> Gatlinburg still would not buy into encouraging a continuation of the program, both because it would require money and a final putting aside of deep-set suspicions that remained from the very beginning. . . . And finally, as things came to [a] critical point, the State of Tennessee hit one of its down periods and tax collections and higher education, along with all state programs, had to eat some of the costs that had originally been budgeted. In the end it pretty much came down to money. . . . But no one could find the money."[7]

Those of us fortunate enough to have worked at this theatre recognize that it shaped our lives in very special ways. We were more or less isolated in the beauty of the Great Smoky Mountains. We were housed and fed, and most of us had technical or management assignments, as well as performance duties. We lived together; we ate together; we performed together. We had to learn to coexist. The experience at Hunter Hills Theatre propelled alumni on to Broadway, to film and television, and into the teaching profession all over the country. All of us can point to the lessons we learned during those glorious summers—lessons of teamwork, responsibility, endurance, and the meaning of rain pace.

As we researched this essay, we realized how important the Hunter Hills experience was to us as artists. Knowing how significant it was to us, we reached out to other alumni of Hunter Hills, and we received dozens of responses. To conclude, we want to share some of these responses, which capture what the Hunter Hills experience meant to hundreds of company members.

Ginny MacColl was a college freshman in 1969 when she was cast as the Dark Witch in *Dark of the Moon*. She made the Knoxville papers when in the course of the performance she accidentally scratched her corneas and had to dance blind on top of the upper stage, which was about twenty feet off the ground. Her testimonial affirms the value of the Hunter Hills experience for preparing aspiring professionals to be successful:

> I realized I'd have to do it blind! Everyone pitched in to make it work. Everyone was there behind me, helping me, watching out for me. And we pulled it off with just a slight brush across the log on center stage as we leaped across it. There's no limit to what actors will accomplish to get the show on! And speaking of *Dark of the Moon*, who wouldn't have etched on their memory the sight of the moon coming out behind the clouds just as Ben said, "Look at the Moon" and the audience all let out a collective gasp. Such a haunting show!
>
> I loved being there. And of course, it shaped my whole life, as I went to NYC to continue dancing and broadened out from there. I worked with Bob Fosse in *Pippin* as a dancer and understudy to Fastrada on B'way. Then branched out to TV commercials and did over 100 National and regional spots.[8]

Richard Stafford, a director and choreographer in New York, shared these thoughts about the Hunter Hills experience, and his words echo Ginny MacColl's:

> I count this as my first paid, professional theatre experience and it helped pave the way or at least further my love of musical theatre. I went on to

> study acting at the London Academy of Music and Dramatic Arts, moved to NYC and have continued to have a career, first as a performer and now as a director and choreographer. The seed was planted at Hunter Hills—I learned how to be a professional there—working as a team to get each show up, stitching costumes, set building and cleaning toilets. I also learned a lot about living 24/7 with those that I was working with, which really helped me in my early touring days. It was a tremendous experience that I look back on with great affection.[9]

Also from New York, Stephanie Weems, general manager of the Magic Circle Opera, shares similar thoughts on her time in the mountains:

> My life and theatrical experiences at Hunter Hills UT Summer Theater Program during the 1960s were pivotal in the development of my career as an artist. . . . With stars in our eyes and stars in the skies, we sang our hearts into the vast expanse of Hunter Hills amphitheatre and dreamed of becoming professional performers. For many of us, our dreams came true and for all of us, we were part of a "magical" artistic community that taught us virtuosity, discipline and the ability to become unstoppable in all aspects of our lives.
>
> From the long hours of rehearsal in the hot sun to the chill of the evening filled with mosquitoes and unexpected storms, we learned to transform our diverse talents and skills into a competent ensemble capable of creating a "real world" on stage. In every drama—onstage and off—we grew-up kicking and screaming, into stronger individuals. These cherished experiences became invaluable lessons that have assisted me throughout my lifelong professional career as a singer, actor and arts administrator.[10]

From Susan Kempainnen, manager of video production of a major hospital, come these comments:

> I'd say that one thing I honed at HH was (given my role as PR coordinator) my organizational skills and a realization of nothing ventured nothing gained. At 20, I was far too young to know what I was doing in the world of public relations . . . creating brochures, calculating the number needed to print, talking with businesses to bring in "restaurant runs," organizing squads of Munchkins to promote *The Wizard of Oz* on the streets of Gatlinburg, etc. Being short of theatrical talent, I came to know that I was talented in other ways that were just as useful to a theatrical company or any organization for that matter.[11]

Ms. Kempainnen's experience at Hunter Hills Theatre confirms the theatre's important role in preparing young people for careers in fields such as marketing, video production, and public relations.

And finally, a note from the late Dan Owenby, teacher, director, and actor, who says, "I was such an innocent when I went to HH, but when I left after two summers I had such confidence and such a wealth of friends who loved theatre like I did. It was a paradise, a party, a place to become what you always wanted to be, a real actor. If I had the chance and the health to do it today, I'd look at my wife and say, 'See ya, honey!'"[12]

As alumni from different summers of Hunter Hills Theatre and as theatre historians, working directors, and academics, we want to ensure that the very special story of Hunter Hills Theatre is preserved. The following is a version of the Hunter Hills Toast, which was composed for the first Hunter Hills Theatre Reunion in 1986. This version is from the most recent reunion in 2006:

With the waters of the Smoky Mountains,
We toast the 50 years of Hunter Hills,
That magical mountain home that first brought us together
And brings us together now.
We toast its memory and our future.
We toast those who cannot be with us,
And those who have gone before us.[13]

Jon Lutz ends his long poem about Hunter Hills with these lines:

We spent our summers learning what makes a friend
We spent our summers not knowing how few here were to spend
We spent our summers like they'd never end
Like no one would ever have to count them
Like none of us would ever be
Just smoke on the mountain.

Notes

1. William J. Morgan to C. Headrick, Feb. 19, 2008.

2. Lorayne Lester, "Re: Need Your Help," email to C. Headrick, Feb. 15, 2008. "And whatever else might be said of Hunter Hills, . . . *Agammenon* [*sic*] was a unique theatrical experience: brilliant acting, directing and the visual effects were so powerful they left the audience breathless for that theatre on that night" (Lester).

3. Howard Richardson and William Berney, *Dark of the Moon* (New York: Theatre Arts Books, 1972), 76.

4. Pat Conroy, *The Prince of Tides* (Boston: Houghton-Mifflin, 1986), 94–95.

5. Lester to Headrick, "Re: Need Your Help."

6. Thomas Cooke, "Any Thoughts," email to C. Headrick, May 3, 2008.

7. Morgan to Headrick, Feb. 19, 2008.

8. Ginny MacColl, "Hunter Hills," email to C. Headrick, Feb. 23, 2008.

9. Richard Stafford, "Re: Hunter Hills," email to C. Headrick, March 27, 2008.

10. Stephanie Weems, "Hunter Hills," email to C. Headrick, Feb. 25, 2008.

11. Susan Kempainnen, "Hunter Hills as a Life Lesson," email to C. Headrick, March 4, 2008.

12. Dan Owenby, "Lost It," email to Michael Russell, April 10, 2008; forwarded to C. Headrick, April 10, 2008.

13. Donald R. Thomas, "Hunter Hills Toast," 1986, revised 2006.

The Promise of Democracy

Imagining National Community in Paul Green's *The Lost Colony*

Angela Sweigart-Gallagher

Outdoor performances were a hallmark of the Federal Theatre Project's attempt to build a "people's theatre" that would bring its disparate American audiences together in order to imagine a national community and to create a regionally dispersed, regionally relevant national theatre. Performances in public parks, amphitheatres, and on portable stages brought drama out of traditional theatre buildings and took it directly to the public. Although a variety of different plays and entertainments were produced for outdoor spaces, patriotic pageants and historical plays made up a significant portion of the Federal Theatre's outdoor offerings. These plays exemplify the Federal Theatre's impulse to use source material from U.S. history, promote American ideals, and call for a return to the promise of America's founding in order to construct a national theatre that would forge an "American" national identity. Paul Green's outdoor historical drama *The Lost Colony*, which was performed in an outdoor amphitheatre on Roanoke Island near the location of the historical "lost colony," offers one example of Federal Theatre playwrights' attempts to use local history as source material and focus in on the lives of average Americans.

S. E. Wilmer contends that the plays and performances by nineteenth- and twentieth-century European national theatres were "important sites for expressing new approaches to national identity." Wilmer observes that in the work of many of these theatres "one can see the attempt to 'awaken the nation' to what is professed to be its natural sense of nationhood and to develop a notion of national character."[1] Like the national theatres in Wilmer's study, the Federal Theatre also attempted to "awaken" its audience(s) to a national identity or character. Green, like many playwrights, directors, and Federal Theatre administrators, sought to reinforce democracy as a fundamental characteristic of the American national community by revisiting and tweaking a familiar theatrical form—the pageant.

Although the large-scale historical pageants promoted by pageant-masters William Chauncy Langdon, Percy MacKaye, and Thomas Wood Stevens had fallen out of favor and were often lampooned by the 1920s, Green drew on many of the techniques of historical pageants from the Progressive Era. In particular, Green seems to have integrated the way in which pageant-masters often used local history as a means to create a sense of national identity and merged sacred and patriotic imagery, while the Federal Theatre's producers followed the pageant model by exhibiting artifacts and recreating important historical sites and integrating members of the local community into the production. By comparison to events such as Langdon's *The Pageant of Indiana* (1916) and MacKay's *The Pageant and Masque of Saint Louis* (1914), the Federal Theatre's production of *The Lost Colony* seems small, and Green presents a much narrower and focused time line than the long series of episodes from a community's founding to its present typical of the Progressive Era pageants. However, what Green, the Federal Theatre administrators, and the Roanoke Island Historical Association seem to have shared with Langdon, his fellow pageant-masters, and Progressive Era promoters of pageants such as the American Pageant Association is the sense that local historical pageants could be used for civic education, as an "instrument of community self-discovery" and a means to "root the spirit of unanimity around a unique local identity."[2] Like the pageant-masters before them, production organizers on *The Lost Colony* hoped that the presentation of Green's fictional account of historical events in the outdoor amphitheatre near the physical location of those events manifested a real and perceived connection to U.S. history and the nation's founding principles. *The Lost Colony* illustrates one way in which the Federal Theatre's historical and patriotic dramas imagined the nation through the staging of American history, mythology, and ideals, and attempted to establish democracy as a fundamental characteristic of American national identity.

Green wrote the play specifically for the Roanoke Island Historical Association in conjunction with a planned anniversary celebration for the 350th year of Virginia Dare's birth, but he and Frederick H. Koch, founder of the Carolina Playmakers at the University of North Carolina and regional adviser to the Federal Theatre, reached out to the Federal Theatre's national office and the WPA for administrative and financial support, as well as theatrical expertise.[3] According to Hallie Flanagan they both felt the "necessity of professional help in casting, lighting,

[and] costuming," as well as "actors, directors, and technicians from Federal Theatre."[4] Flanagan happily provided this support, and in turn the Federal Theatre was able to claim *The Lost Colony*'s debut in July 1937 and the production in general as a crowning achievement for the Federal Theatre, and the development of sites on Roanoke and the building of the Waterside Theatre as a similar achievement of the WPA and the Civilian Conservation Corps (CCC).

As the play's title suggests, Green loosely based *The Lost Colony* on Sir Walter Raleigh's attempt to establish a permanent British colony in the New World. Through narration and pantomime in the first few scenes, Green depicts the landing of the first wave of settlers, their initial cooperation with the Native Americans, and subsequent conflict with local tribes. The realistic scenes that follow focus on Raleigh's presentation of gifts to Queen Elizabeth (including Wanchese and Manteo, two Indians taken back to England) and his attempts to gain permission and resources for the permanent colony. Elizabeth grants permission for a permanent colony, with the caveat that Raleigh would remain to aid her in the impending war with Spain, and Raleigh puts together a motley crew for a second wave of settlers. This crew includes the play's "all-American" hero, John Borden; the beautiful heroine, Eleanor Dare, along with her foppish husband, Ananias Dare; a drunk beggar known as old Tom; and the notably foreign villain, Simon Fernando. On arriving at the settlement, John, Eleanor, and the rest of the colonists discover that Indians have killed all of the first wave of settlers, and Wanchese realizes his father has been murdered by those settlers during his voyage to England. Wanchese vows revenge and flees the colony to return to his people. Manteo remains with the colonists and endeavors to help them as they struggle to survive. As the colonists approach starvation, with their stores and energies running low, a runner arrives to announce the presence of a Spanish ship offshore. Faced with the possibility of a battle with the Spanish "invaders," the colonists choose to face their fate in the wilderness and abandon the settlement they had fought so hard to protect.

The Lost Colony as National Memorial: Merging Patriotic and Religious Imagery

Although Green referred to *The Lost Colony* as a symphonic drama, rather than a pageant, *The Lost Colony* has clear connections with the pageant movement and to the pageants put forth by noted pageant-masters such as MacKaye, Langdon, and Thomas Wood Stevens. Like its pageant predecessors from the Progressive Era, *The Lost Colony* used history and historical imagery as a means to define a sense of national identity. As David Glassberg has observed, public historical imagery such as that in *The Lost Colony* not only has the power to "define a common understanding of experience"; it also serves to help shape culture.[5] Green used the local history of Fort Raleigh as a means to reflect what he saw as the national community's democratic identity, as well as to shape the audience's perception about the colony's national importance. Green's text, in conjunction with the physical production at the Waterside Theatre on Roanoke Island, and the Federal Theatre's buildup to and promotion of the play, created a national celebration of and memorial to the fallen pioneers of the Roanoke Colony, the goal of which was to create and foster a shared sense of national community among its audience.

Despite the failure of the colony, Green manages to create a play that is solemn yet hopeful about the future of American democracy. Echoing the civic celebrations of the late nineteenth century that served as the basis for later pageants, Green emphasizes the spiritual connection of the modern nation to this early, failed colony by merging religious and patriotic imagery, an idea exemplified by a photograph of a chapel reconstructed on the island by the WPA and an accompanying caption printed in the 1937 program. The photograph depicts Saint George's Cross and the American flag hanging over the altar, and the accompanying caption suggests that the reconstructed chapel "epitomizes the religious note in the celebration."[6]

In his discussion of the many centennial celebrations of 1876, Glassberg identifies the centrality of a historical oration to the festivities, which was "set like a sermon amid a program of invocations, hymns, and benedictions."[7] Interestingly, *The Lost Colony* mimics these civic celebrations in the opening scene with an invocation and prayer sung by a chorus and led by a "Minister." A chorus fills the stage and sings out: "O God that madest earth and sky and hedged the restless seas around, who that vast firmament on high . . . O God our Father, Lord above . . . secure within Thy boundless love we walk this way of death alone." Incidentally, this same song and choral staging ends the play. The Minister joins the chorus onstage and (from his spotlight) appeals to God to witness the dedication of this sacred land that he—and presumably the cast, crew, and audience—have come to provide. I say "presumably" because the notion of "We," used by the Minister, is never clearly defined in the script. The Minister calls out to God but, more important, to the assembled audience: "We ask the witness of thy grace upon this sacred spot, this bit of humble earth we have come to dedicate." The Minister dedicates this spot in the name of "the men of dreams, the sons of hope and pain and wonder." He describes himself and the audience as the "children who came after them" for whom these "men of dreams" cried, "O land majestic, free, unbounded." The message of the chorus and the Minister is that the dream, the "vision" that propelled the pioneers to tackle the New World, lives on and "shall not die."[8]

The Minister's ideas are echoed by the "Speaker," who seconds the notion that the play is a dedication to both the colonists' sacrifices and a dedication to the nation. The Speaker addresses the audience directly, "Friends, we are gathered here this evening to honor the spiritual birthplace of our nation," and in a feature later cut from future productions, a "Historian" guides the audience to an interpretation of the events as they begin. The Historian opens with, "In the time of Queen Elizabeth many men and women, notably among them Sir Walter Raleigh, continued their dream of founding an English speaking colony in the new world." As events unfold, the Historian interrupts the action to make further comment on the significance of certain events. Prior to the final choral invocation and prayer, the Historian offers his own final thought, "And so the Lost Colony made ready to leave the fort, driving themselves on with the last gasp of energy. . . . In the cold hours before dawn the colonists began their march into the unknown wilderness."[9]

The religious vision and faith of the pioneers is intimately tied up with their desire to create a new nation and a "new form of government," and Green weaves these two ideas throughout the play. The Minister and the Speaker render the theatre a civic chapel, a means to celebrate and embrace the message of hope that manages to pervade the play, despite the presumed death of its main characters. The idea of "keeping faith," and of paying homage to the fallen colonists raised by the Minister and Speaker in the first scene, resonates throughout the script and throughout the experience of attending the production.[10]

Just as the audience is asked to keep faith, the colonists themselves also continually (re)affirm their faith in the new colony and their dream of a new nation. Even as the colony's plight becomes ever direr, Eleanor and John Borden hold on to the desires for a freer, more democratic nation. As the colony's reverend falls ill, Eleanor and Borden share a private moment in which they agree to abandon the fort so that the colony may survive and carry on. The two reaffirm their faith in the colonial mission and their dream of a new nation:

> BORDEN: Thus we agree—we two, standing here tonight upon the outpost of the world, the last survivors—keepers of a dream.
> ELEANOR: (Murmuring.) A dream!
> BORDEN: And we'll keep that dream—keep it to the end!
> ELEANOR: Yes, together we will.[11]

After the two, along with their fellow colonists, decide to leave the fort, Borden reminds the assembled colonists that they "leave the fort only to return again." In doing so, Borden suggests the possibility of hope and renewal despite the obvious fact that the fort was abandoned and the colonists "lost." According to the National Park Service's official Web site, for the "depression-weary audiences of the thirties, *The Lost Colony* represented their own journey through hardship." If this supposition is true, then for the audience, like the colonists, the march through the wilderness at the end of the play offered a moment of hope: "The unknown was still ahead, but perhaps the worst was over."[12]

The Lost Colony as National Passion Play

As the ceremonial opening scene suggests, in *The Lost Colony* Green reflects the political and religious aspects of the colonists' mission. This merging of sacred, national, and theatrical was not only a reflection of pageant tradition but also a reflection of Green's interest in creating a North Carolinian *Oberammergau.* Green's play was heavily influenced by Oberammergau's Passion play, which was as much a civic celebration as a religious one. According to John E. Tailby, Oberammergau's Passion play began when "following a severe outbreak of the Black Death in 1633, the inhabitants of this Upper Bavarian village vowed to perform a Passion play every ten years if they were spared from further deaths."[13] Like *The Lost Colony,* the ongoing production of *Oberammergau* celebrates the continuance of a civic community despite the hardships endured by its inhabitants. The Federal Theatre likewise acknowledged and even highlighted the influence of *Oberammergau* in the commemorative programs produced for the first two years of production. In an article entitled "The Growth of an Epic Drama," an unnamed author writes of the debut in 1937: "Thousands of visitors hailed *The Lost Colony* as the greatest native American drama ever produced. Critics called it the patriotic *Oberammergau* of America."[14] In fact, critics did relate the production to *Oberammergau,* and they expected their readership to be familiar with the significance of that connection. Writing for the *Baltimore Evening Sun,* Gerald W. Johnson called on his readers to "imagine an entirely secular Oberammergau" so that they might "have some conception of the psychic state of Manteo, NC."[15]

Green's play and its production at the Waterside Theatre on Roanoke Island not only share the religious-civic celebratory aspect of Oberammergau's Passion play; it also shares some similarities with North American Passion plays. These similarities suggest some of the means by which the production imagined an American national community. In her essay on North American Passion plays, Dorothy Chansky suggests that Passion plays speak "to a large imagined community—Christians of many denominations—in locally inflected ways."[16] Likewise, Green's play and its production at the Waterside Theatre on Roanoke Island spoke to a large imagined community of Americans in both a practical and spiritual sense, using local historical events as the raw material. On the practical side, *The Lost Colony* was a regional production, but to succeed, the production had to pull its audience from the American community at large. The Federal Theatre, along with the Roanoke Colony Memorial Association of Manteo and other WPA projects, helped reinvent Roanoke Island as a tourist destination for just that purpose.

In terms of the spiritual aspect, the play also spoke to a large imagined community of Americans through its patriotic message, which like that of a Passion play speaks largely to a community of those already converted but does so in a form that suggests a proselytizing mission. The conversion or reaffirmation of faith that Chansky describes as the proposed mission or hope of many producers of traditional Passion plays is transformed in *The Lost Colony.* Here audience members were asked to affirm a spiritual connection with the sacrifice and bravery of the settlers and take in the play's patriotic message. That message seems to be that the bravery and belief in a "new nation" and a "new form of government" guided the colony from its start. In *Arena* Flanagan recounts a conversation with Green in which he said, "Everyone looking for someone in America is a spiritual descendant of those men flooding across the sea. Not just good men and great—all sorts of men—rich men, poor men, beggar men, thieves—the weak of will, the hard of fist—all seeking a new place, a free place, a wider scope for their endeavor and their dream." This notion of a spiritual connection with the lost colony was picked up by Roosevelt himself. The commemorative programs quote Roosevelt as saying, "We do not know the fate of Virginia Dare or the first colony. We do know, however, that the story of America is largely a record of that spirit of adventure" and the "fruition of their brave endeavor."[17] In essence, Green's and Roosevelt's statements frame the pioneers as martyrs to the American project.

Old World versus New: Claims of Cultural Heritage and New Identities

Throughout the first act of the play, Green's characters refer to the visions and dreams they have for a new nation, the essence of which is a focus on the people and democracy. These dreams for a new nation support Green's attempts to define the colony as the first step toward modern American democracy and, at the same time, create an interesting conflict or tension with his attempts to define the Roanoke Colony as an extension of England and English law and civilization. In the script this tension begins with an attempt to reframe Queen Elizabeth's power as dependent on the people rather than being bestowed on her by God. In scene three a beggar and a soldier exchange words about Sir Walter Raleigh's attempts to begin a colony in the New World. The Beggar claims that Sir Walter Raleigh "was once poor himself, and may be so again. Likewise the Queen." The Soldier challenges the assertion that the queen is poor because she represents "the height of heaven's favor." The Beggar dissents: "As the world knows the queen's power depends on the poor people, and the common people are all poor." Referring to himself and poor people like him, the Beggar notes: "Never will he [Sir Walter Raleigh] make a colony on Roanoke except through us. It is now the time of the demos—that's Greek for it—democracy, the rule of the people."[18] While the Beggar claims the source of Queen Elizabeth's power lies with the poor people who support her, the new colony extends and expands the role and power of the people. In this way Green attempts to rhetorically link the colony with England while simultaneously setting it apart.

Sir Walter Raleigh provides another moment of tension between Green's depiction of the colony as an extension of England and as the first step toward a new nation. Throughout the play Elizabeth and Raleigh disagree about the importance of providing support to the colony at Roanoke in relation to the importance of conserving resources for the impending war with Spain. Elizabeth requires some convincing to allow Eleanor, John Borden, and the others to set out on their journey. Raleigh attempts to prove to Elizabeth the necessity of establishing a colony on Roanoke by providing an analogy between trees and nations: "There is an ancient saying that if a tree would grow great it must send its roots deep and wide. In its shade the lesser trees will die. So it is with nations, so with an idea, or by your leave, a dream."[19] Ostensibly, Raleigh seems to be discussing the British Empire and its need to send its roots deep and wide into the "New World." However, in this passage Raleigh also refers to the nation as an "idea" or as a "dream," which echoes the dreams of the pioneering colonists to establish a new nation, referenced in the play's first scene and opening dedication.

Articles and promotional materials shared the play's tension between the concept of Roanoke Island as the "first English colony," as it was often described in articles and on park placards, and the depiction of Roanoke as the "birthplace of the nation," as the colony was advertised in other articles and fliers. The most interesting example of this refrain was the Carolina Coach Company's attempts to market its bus trips to and from the island. A handbill pasted into the Federal Theatre Scrapbook held in the University of North Carolina's collection, advertises itself in the handbill's headline as the "Connecting Link from ALL AMERICA to Roanoke Island" and "North Carolina's and America's 350th Anniversary Celebration at the Birthplace of the Nation." In the advertisement's smaller text the handbill describes Roanoke Island as the "Cradle of the Nation's Birth . . . where Sir Walter Raleigh's intrepid colonists founded the first Anglo-American settlement."[20]

Ultimately Green and the Federal Theatre, as well as the promotional departments of local businesses, present the colony on Roanoke Island as having a claim to the cultural heritage of the British Empire, while still separating itself as something leading to a distinct nation, separated by its enduring belief in freedom and democracy.[21]

The Physical Surroundings and National Celebration as Context

The production's unique performance site, an outdoor amphitheatre advertised as the historical site of Sir Walter Raleigh's lost colony and part of a larger exhibit of lost colony sites and artifacts, imbued the production with the aura of a national shrine, where audience members walked the hallowed ground on which the original colonists once walked, lived, and may have even died. In conjunction with the planned production, federal resources poured into Roanoke Island to build Waterside Theatre and restore Fort Raleigh to its "authentic condition." In an article for *Backstage*, a publication of the North Carolina Federal Theatre Project edited by Koch, Koch writes about the scheduled premiere of *The Lost Colony:* "The original Fort Raleigh, the huddle of thatched cabins and little log chapel where Virginia Dare was baptized, have been authentically reconstructed by the Works Progress Administration."[22] The notion of "authentic condition," or "original site" loomed large in the language of the Federal Theatre and everyone else involved in the production, and it seems to have been part of a larger strategy to encourage audiences to identify with the colonists depicted in the play and create a sense of hallowed ground.

The Federal Theatre's commemorative program materials from 1937 and 1938 contain multiple images of the recreated fort and chapel, including an image of two children in front of the reconstructed fort with the bolded caption, "The fort is rebuilt on the *original* site" (my emphasis), followed by a longer description in smaller font. This longer description describes the "blockhouse" as being "built of rough juniper logs, hewn by hand with an adz on the grounds" and notes that in 1654 Francis Yeardley, a Virginia minister, wrote about a young man who ventured to Roanoke while on a hunting exhibition. As the Yeardley quotation indicates, while at Roanoke, the young hunter "found the great commander of those parts with his Indians a hunting, who received them civilly, shewed [*sic*] them the ruins of Sir Walter Raleigh's fort, from whence I received a sure token of their being there." This caption and the sourceless quotation from Yeardley are presented as evidence of the accurate reconstruction and placement of the fort.[23]

The fact that audience members had to walk across the island, through the "abandoned settlement," to get to the performance space physically connected the Federal Theatre's audience to the lives and hardships of the colonists. As audiences walked through the island to the theatre, they could observe the buildings and imposing forest and imagine the lives of colonists in the same way that the contemporary museum exhibits at Monticello and other historical heritage museums serve to offer visitors an opportunity to imagine the lives of former inhabitants through the architectural artifacts "left behind" or, in this case, reconstructed. The reconstructed buildings on Roanoke Island served a similar purpose to the one Glassberg identifies in his discussion of the demarcation of significant locations by the local historical society at the centennial celebration of General Burgoyne's surrender in Schuylerville, New York, held in 1887. The reconstructed buildings and their display by the Federal Theatre and the local historical society transformed Roanoke Island into a "ceremonial landscape imbued with sacred significance."[24]

Similarly, the audience's "pilgrimage," as Flanagan referred to the journey across the sound and through the island in *Arena*, served to remind the audience of the colonists' own journey and experience of the natural elements of the island. By touring the village and imagining the lives of the colonists, Federal Theatre audiences were reminded of the struggles and sacrifices made by the colonists in order to establish the democratic nation so triumphantly celebrated in the play. Flanagan describes Roanoke Island as "affording a natural stage," which for her consisted of "the forest, the cabins in the clearing, the fort, the chapel, the slope on the waterside."[25] The entire island, the recreated colony, and the Waterside Theatre melded, making each aspect at once a chapel, a national shrine, and a national theatre in which the lives of the colonists were enacted, remembered, and celebrated.

The Federal Theatre and the local parties involved in the production heightened the experience of the production and the island as a national shrine for the audience(s) by framing the play and its production within a larger government-sponsored and government-endorsed celebration through promotional efforts. Federal Theatre press releases from the Education Section of the Department of Information stress the wider scope of the project. One press release begins by noting that Green wrote the play specifically for the "two-month celebration of the 350th anniversary of Virginia Dare's birth." The release also stresses the extent to which many federal groups came together to present the production: "The WPA Federal Theatre will aid in the celebration by furnishing actors for the play while the WPA Federal Music Project's North Carolina State Symphony Orchestra will play a special score written for the production."[26] Local and regional papers such as the *Dare County Times*, the *Durham Sun*, and the *Norfolk Ledger* seem to have picked up Federal Theatre press releases such as the one quoted above. They published dozens of articles, photographs, and even cartoons about the colony's history, the reconstruction of the colony, the construction of the theatre, and Green's play. Newspaper articles also appeared in papers outside of the Roanoke area, including papers with national distribution. Many of these articles focused on the lengths to which the government had gone to recreate the colony. For example, on October 11, 1936, a photographic essay entitled "America's 'Lost Colony' Restored; 350-Year-Old Unsolved Mystery" appeared in the Sunday edition of the *New York Times*. Notably, the article's title is not "North Carolina's" Lost Colony. Rather, the unnamed author stresses that the Lost Colony belongs to America. The author places Roanoke's importance alongside the "patriotic shrines" of Jamestown and Plymouth, while acknowledging that it "remains largely forgotten," at least until the reconstruction began.[27] The photographs accompanying the article are the same photographs that appear in the commemorative playbills for the 1937 and 1938 productions of *The Lost Colony*.

In another move to publicize the national celebration surrounding the premiere, Federal Theatre officials highlighted the participation of other governmental agencies. Koch, in his article for *Backstage*, advertised the creation of a commemorative coin in conjunction with the production. The coin, produced by the Philadelphia mint, featured Eleanor holding an infant Virginia Dare on one side and Sir Walter Raleigh on the other side, suggesting the wide scope of celebratory activity. The 1937 program distributed at the production also contained images of the coin, noting that it was modeled on two Roanoke Islanders, Mrs. S. S. McKee and her daughter Anne Laurie. While the issuance of the coin, along with a number of other activities such as an essay contest geared toward high school students, was technically outside the scope of the Federal Theatre, the fact that Federal Theatre administrators promoted these activities (and later compiled evidence of them) suggests that these administrators construed them as part of a larger national celebration of which the production of Green's *The Lost Colony* was only one part.[28]

The commemorative programs provide a glimpse of how the Federal Theatre saw the activities of the different federal and local agencies coming together to create a total experience for the audience. Franklin Roosevelt's widely publicized attendance that first year on August 18, the birthday of Virginia Dare, legitimized the production's national significance. Headshots of administrators from the WPA, Federal Theatre, and other federal agencies throughout 1937 and 1938 reminded the audience of the federal government's involvement with and sponsorship of the production. Articles and photographs also detailed the extent to which the production was a collaboration of the Federal Theatre, the Roanoke Island Historical Association, and the Carolina Playmakers. In the 1938 program Samuel Selden, who directed both the first and second season of *The Lost Colony,* describes the production as "communal theatre" because of the way in which so many groups and individuals came together to create the production. Newspaper articles appearing prior to the premiere advertised that local musicians were employed to provide accompanying music.[29]

In many ways it is this communal aspect that most aligns *The Lost Colony* with the historical pageants of Langdon, MacKaye, and Stevens. While maintaining necessary Federal Theatre standards about the professional status of actors on the production, the Federal Theatre's attempts to integrate local groups into the production was evident and became the basis of Flanagan's claims about *The Lost Colony* as an example of when "a play becomes a philosophic and poetic concept of the way a democracy can work" and of when the theatre becomes "not a private affair, but a public experience, in which mature workers in all the arts join with the citizens in all walks of life to create dramatic celebrations which at once illumine and enrich our American heritage."[30] In presenting the play as part of a larger national and patriotic celebration, the Federal Theatre's production of *The Lost Colony* provided audiences with an image of the American national community as being, from the moment of its birth, steeped in the ideals of democracy and invited its audience(s) to identify themselves with characters and with the ideals of democracy and freedom represented onstage.

The Lost Colony also served as a model for the way in which other Federal Theatre units could incorporate local history and traditions into a national theatre based on regionally dispersed and specific theatrical activities. Although perhaps the most successful example, *The Lost Colony* was not the only Federal Theatre attempt to use local history as source material. Federal Theatres in almost every region of the country engaged in attempts to stage and eventually write plays and pageants that addressed local history, particularly when that local history had national consequences. For example, after John McGee's play *Jefferson Davis* failed abysmally in its Broadway debut, Flanagan encouraged Federal Theatres throughout the South to put on the play, presuming it would have broader appeal for southern audiences. She appears to have been right. It played in Chapel Hill, North Carolina, and across the South, where it apparently fared much better than on Broadway. The headline of one review, which appeared in the *Raleigh Times,* summarizes the general press reaction; it read, "Davis Play Outstanding."[31]

Plays submitted in one region or in one state were often redirected to specific directors because a given play would likely appeal to audiences within that region or state. For example, the Federal Theatre's Play Bureau sent John Hunter Booth's *Created Equal,* a play about the development and subsequent amendments to the Constitution, to Herbert Humphreys, State Director Pennsylvania, and Charles LaRue, State Director Connecticut, in consideration of a simultaneous regional production in part because the play contained scenes depicting regional and local historical events such as the Whiskey Rebellion. *Jefferson Davis* and *Created Equal* are not the same kind of history play as *The Lost Colony* in that they are not site-specific outdoor dramas produced as part of a larger patriotic celebration. However, all three share the impulse to use local and regional history as source material for making the Federal Theatre a cultural institution relevant to various audiences. Like *The Lost Colony,* these plays and many other history plays written and produced by the Federal Theatre tied local history into a national narrative about American history and American identity.

The history produced in *The Lost Colony* focuses on the role of the average American in establishing the nation. Flanagan recounts a conversation she had with Green: "He went on to say that historical plays should concern themselves not with the leading characters of history but the surge of common men and women who make history though they are seldom recorded in it."[32] This focus on the often-unnamed characters of history is repeated throughout the plays written and produced by the Federal Theatre Project. Plays such as *Created Equal* and the living newspapers all demonstrate the effects of history on the daily lives of Americans. Even when Federal Theatre plays did consider the lives of national heroes as their subject, Federal Theatre playwrights often did so in a way that highlighted the commonness of these heroes. In other words, these plays stressed that national heroes were just like any other American. In *The Lost Colony* Queen Elizabeth, Sir Walter Raleigh, and Governor John White are all characters in the play, but Green focuses on the lives (and possible deaths) of Eleanor Dare, Virginia Dare, Old Tom, and the other colonists depicted in the play. Although these characters are largely at the mercy of choices made by the larger characters, Green's drama focuses in on their daily lives, hardships, bravery, and sacrifices.

Ultimately, *The Lost Colony* was not only a model for Federal Theatre productions and plays but also a metaphor for the entire Federal Theatre Project and its efforts to establish a national theatre. In *Arena* Flanagan concludes her discussion of Federal Theatre activities in the South by acknowledging that the plan to create a regional southern theatre in Chapel Hill was "still under discussion in Washington when the project ended." Rather than despair about these thwarted efforts, however, Flanagan ends with the following observation: "Those of us who worked on it should realize it does not matter through what agency plans finally get carried out. Other colonists will come." In the same way that Green's final scene seemed hopeful because, as Flanagan notes, "the colonists continued to believe in the principles on which their colony was established—freedom, justice, and goodwill," Flanagan saw opportunities to be hopeful about America's theatrical future as a result of her experience working on *The Lost Colony*.[33]

Notes

1. S. E. Wilmer, "Reifying Imagined Communities: Nationalism, Post-Colonialism, and Theatre Historiography," *Nordic Studies* 12 (1999): 94–103.

2. David Glassberg, *American Historical Pageantry: The Uses of Tradition in the Early Twentieth Century* (Chapel Hill: University of North Carolina Press, 1990), 72, 75.

3. Shortly after accepting the position at the University of North Carolina, Koch wrote and helped stage a pageant entitled *Raleigh: The Shepherd of the Ocean* (1918). Koch's interest in what he called "folk drama," which seems to have included pageants, largely shaped the Federal Theatre's activities in North Carolina.

4. Hallie Flanagan, *Arena* (New York: Duell, Sloan and Pearce, 1940), 111.

5. Glassberg, *American Historical Pageantry,* 1–2.

6. *The Lost Colony* souvenir program, July 1937, 4.

7. Glassberg, *American Historical Pageantry,* 9.

8. Paul Green, *The Lost Colony: A Symphonic Drama in Two Acts (With Music, Pantomime, and Dance)* (Chapel Hill: University of North Carolina Press, 1939), 5–6.

9. Ibid., 6.

10. Ibid., 5–6.

11. Ibid., 129.

12. Fort Raleigh National Historic Site, "*The Lost Colony:* A Cure for Depression?" www.nps.gov/archive/fora/div_col.htm (accessed Jan. 13, 2008).

13. John E. Tailsby, "Oberammergau," in *The Cambridge Guide to Theatre,* ed. Martin Banham (New York: Cambridge University Press, 1992), 723.

14. "The Growth of Epic Drama," *The Lost Colony* souvenir program, July 1938, 3.

15. Gerald W. Johnson, "Story of Missing Colony Told in National Setting on North Carolina Coast," *Baltimore Sun,* July 21, 1937, clipping in Federal Theatre Scrapbook, vol. 1, 1935–1937, North Carolina Collection, University of North Carolina at Chapel Hill.

16. Dorothy Chansky, "North American Passion Plays: 'The Greatest Story Ever Told' in the New Millennium," *TDR* 50, no. 4 (Winter 2006): 120–45, 122.

17. Flanagan, *Arena,* 111; *The Lost Colony* souvenir program, July 1937, 2; *The Lost Colony* souvenir program, July 1938, 2.

18. Green, *The Lost Colony,* 20–21.

19. Ibid., 30.

20. Johnson, "Story of Missing Colony Told in Natural Setting on North Carolina Coast"; Carolina Coach Company Handbill, in Federal Theatre Scrapbook, vol. 1, 1935–1937, North Carolina Collection, University of North Carolina at Chapel Hill.

21. In an odd moment that is cut from later versions of the play, that heritage includes William Shakespeare, who meets Raleigh and asks to be allowed to join the colonists in their endeavors.

22. Frederick Koch, "*The Lost Colony* on Roanoke Island," *Backstage* 2, no. 7 (no date): 2. While Federal Theatre officials and the Roanoke Island Historical Association stressed the authenticity of the reconstructed fort in their print materials, the National Park Service was unhappy with the reconstruction. However, the National Park Service's protest does not seem to have had a large impact on the way the work at Roanoke Island was viewed by critics and journalists, nor did it impact the way in which the fort was represented to the public.

23. "The Fort Is Rebuilt on the Original Site," *The Lost Colony* souvenir program, July 1938, 31.

24. Glassberg, American Historical Pageantry, 14.

25. Flanagan, *Arena,* 111.

26. Press release for *The Lost Colony,* n.d., in Federal Theatre Scrapbook, vol. 1, 1935–1937, North Carolina Collection, University of North Carolina at Chapel Hill.

27. "America's 'Lost Colony'; 350-Year-Old Unsolved Mystery," *New York Times,* Oct. 11, 1936.

28. *The Lost Colony* souvenir program, July 1937, 28. The commemorative coin advertisement and the pamphlet for *The Lost Colony* essay contest are in the Federal Theatre Scrapbook, vol. 1, 1935–1937, North Carolina Collection, University of North Carolina at Chapel Hill.

29. See "Roanoke People Play for Drama," undated clipping, Federal Theatre Scrapbook, vol. 1, 1935–1937, North Carolina Collection, University of North Carolina at Chapel Hill.

30. Flanagan, *Arena,* 112.

31. See "Davis Play Outstanding," *Raleigh Times,* March 17, 1936, Federal Theatre Scrapbook, vol. 1, 1935–1937, North Carolina Collection, University of North Carolina at Chapel Hill.

32. Flanagan, *Arena,* 112.

33. Ibid., 111, 112, 113.

The Revitalization of Space

Freestyle Parkour and Its Audiences

Jeanmarie Higgins

On the Saturday of the 2008 SETC Theatre Symposium on outdoor performance, conference presenters gathered for lunch at the Forest Theatre on the University of North Carolina campus at Chapel Hill to attend an informal talk from keynote speaker Scott Parker, former director of the Institute of Outdoor Drama. Parker recounted the history of the theatre site, a stone outdoor amphitheatre used to stage dramas in the outdoors since 1916. This talk was one of a set of events that generated discussion about the breadth of material the phrase *outdoor performance* embraces, from the outdoor historical dramas of Roanoke's *The Lost Colony* to American railroad pageants, from the potential theatricality of found outdoor urban spaces such as Deborah Warner's New York City *Angel Project* to self-consciously intrusive forms like guerilla theatre and my own work on the dance/sport parkour. A serendipitous collision of two forms of outdoor performance occurred at lunch that day. As we listened to Parker, two young men—dressed head to toe in black—appeared at the top of the audience seating and began to run downhill through the theatre. They bounded past us, down the stepped seating, leaping from level to level, the group of scholars eating lunch just another set of obstacles to navigate. When they reached the bottom of the hill, they ran upstage, exited the theatre, vaulted a picnic bench, and disappeared into the surrounding woods. "Was that parkour?" someone asked.

This essay explores the dance/sport freestyle parkour from its beginnings as a group activity—an activity that, according to its practitioners, is "all about community and development"—to its later media construction as a countercultural solo urban practice associated with lawlessness, danger, and domination. All types of outdoor performance have one element in common, an audience—an audience that does not exist, as Herbert Blau has illustrated in his many works concerning the limits of performance, "until it is *thought*."[1] This essay further considers the audiences of parkour, the audience called into spectatorship by the parkour "interruption" at the Forest Theatre, and the audience of consumers served by the representations of parkour generated by various media. This essay will examine how spectatorship—the live spectatorship of the kind we experienced in the Forest Theatre, and the mediated spectatorship generated by photographs and films—shapes the perception of parkour.

Parkour began as an activity practiced in suburbs, but as its commercial visibility—and potential for commodification—grew, representations of the sport were set in more "interesting," urban places. Popular understanding of parkour has been shaped by the media's desire to connect it to the city and encourages consumers of these representations to view parkour as a critique of the totalizing strategies of these cities. At the same time, the everyday practice of parkour—the Forest Theatre free-run being an instance—while easily seen as a critique of capitalist spaces, can also precipitate this dance/sport into a condition of theatre by shifting a crowd's attention into a (perhaps unexpected) scopic consumption of the performer's movement through space.

Parkour: An Introduction

Frequently called "skateboarding without a skateboard,"[2] parkour practitioners, called *traceurs*,[3] partner with rural, suburban, and urban spaces to perform seamless improvised movement built from a set of more or less codified moves. Unlike free-runners, who mine an outdoor site for its potential before moving on, traceurs travel. According to parkour founder David Belle, "Parkour is an art that helps you pass any obstacle to go from point A to point B using only the abilities of the human body."[4] Traceurs scale and climb, duck under and jump over the obstacles they encounter, charting as straight a path as possible, without losing momentum, in the most beautiful way possible. Key to parkour is "flow," which according to one traceur is "like water flowing down stream and coming up to a boulder. Instead of smashing into it, the water simply moves around it and continues its journey."[5]

As meditative as the pursuit of "flow" might sound, parkour is an intensely physical practice. Training is required to master parkour's demanding moves, which include running up walls, balancing on railings, and jumping from rooftop to rooftop. Nonetheless, the primary goal of parkour is not to execute awe-inspiring stunts but to cover ground as quickly as possible despite obstacles. According to one traceur, "It is well to remember that anything unmoving in nature is already dead or dying. At its heart, parkour is about growth and about development, both on a personal level and as a community. In short, it is about movement."[6] Parkour has much in common with site-specific dance and with contact improvisation. Traceurs build their runs from a set of skills—vaults and jumps appropriate for specific kinds of obstacles like railings, gaps between buildings, or walls without handholds.[7] And the traceur's relationship to obstacles is similar to the relationship of dancers to other dancers in contact improvisation, who "keep their energy freely flowing . . . basing their improvisation on the physical forces of weight and momentum."[8]

Parkour is difficult to describe without addressing its correspondences with other kinetic forms including dance, martial arts, and military training. Developed in a suburb of Paris in the 1980s by David Belle, parkour is based on moves and techniques Belle learned from his father, a French Vietnam War veteran who refined the practice from *parcours du combatant*—the obstacle-course-based military training outlined by early twentieth-century naval officer George Hébert. The word *parkour* is a neologism constructed from the French term for course, *parcours*, the letter *c* replaced with a *k* to emphasize the activity's aggressive nature, and the silent *s* omitted to reflect parkour's demand for efficiency. Parkour is commonly considered to fall under the set of practices called "infiltration," or "urban exploration in areas not designed for public usage."[9] Although preceded by and related to skateboarding, surfing, site-specific dance, theatre, performance art, and martial arts, parkour occupies a space somewhere between sport and dance, between athleticism and grace, practice and performance. Relating parkour to one set of practices leads the interpreter to relate it to yet another. This hybridity makes parkour resistant to categorization and to truthful representations in the popular media.

Early representations of parkour in mainstream media were true to the practice's sense of play, if not to its usual place of performance. Parkour grew in visibility in 2002 with the BBC1 promotional film, *Rush Hour*, where a bare-chested David Belle free-runs through London, rooftop to rooftop, to arrive home in time to watch his favorite television show. Underscored by Michael Bublé's cover of Dean Martin's "Sway,"[10] this advertisement shows Belle as an overworked businessman "getting one over" on the strategy of the London city plan—"flying" home while the ordinary commuters on the street wait at crowded crosswalks or lean on their car horns in standstill traffic. The following year, the BBC aired *Jump London,* a series of videos featuring Belle's friend and parkour cofounder Sebastien Foucan. *Jump London* features Foucan and others free-running among familiar London sites. Representations of parkour are becoming more common, especially as they are incorporated into other forms of entertainment, such as music videos[11] and popular films—the most well known being the Daniel Craig–Sebastien Foucan chase sequence in the 2006 remake of the James Bond movie *Casino Royale.*[12]

Parkour as Practice: Revitalizing the Waste Spaces of City Planning

Parkour invites a range of theoretical interpretations, all of which address the individual's relationship to a planned environment. Parkour can be seen as one of the "infinitesimal procedures, which have not been 'privileged' by history" that Michel de Certeau proposes in *The Practice of Everyday Life,* the traceur pursuing his or her "silent itinerary" as an act of protest against the technologies of power he or she can do nothing to change.[13] Parkour can be read as performances of situationist *détournement,* as Henri Lefebvre uses the term to describe how youth repurpose underused civic spaces into "places of play."[14] David Thomson theorizes parkour directly, positioning the traceur as an embodiment of the "figure of the wanderer" in the space of what he terms "capital city."[15] Before parkour reached a wide audience of culture consumers, it was practiced primarily on the outskirts of cities, in the forgotten places of failed planning projects analogous to what Jane Jacobs calls "border vacuums"—areas unused owing to planners' failure to consider how users navigate space. These are places we recognize not as singular sites but as familiar instances of failed community planning—a concrete amphitheatre outside a new library that no one uses as a proper performance space, a staircase from a train station platform that leads nowhere, or a park Jacobs might describe as "deprived of life": "for people do confer use on parks and make them successes—or else withhold use and doom parks to rejection and failure.[16] Seen in this way, traceurs reimagine the places city planners have created for everyday users, creating ephemeral works of skill and beauty in forgotten territory.

In *Skateboarding, Space, and the City* the architecture scholar Iain Borden argues that urban sports like skateboarding critique the places capitalist space has created: "Where capitalism sub-divides and controls, measures and turns land into a commodity—skaters . . . adopt and exploit a given physical terrain in order to present . . . new and distinctive uses other than the original function of that terrain."[17] The skater Craig

Stecyk echoes Borden's idea as he summarizes the role skaters play in revitalizing spaces: "Skaters by their very nature are urban guerillas: they make everyday use of the useless artifacts of the technological burden, and employ the handiwork of the government/corporate structure in a thousand ways that the original architects could never dream of."[18] Although certain parallels are relevant, parkour's relationship to skateboarding and urban infiltration is generally overstated, especially its connection to trespassing and other illegal acts. An urban explorer spends time with a site, must trespass in order to gain access to it, and is usually interested in the site's history.[19] Traceurs, by definition, keep moving and do not focus on the obstacles in their way for longer than it takes to size them up: "Parkour is about using whatever is in front of you, it is not your problem to worry how it got there or if it should even be there or not, just how you use it, how you interact with it; . . . the discipline shuns the built environment and its imposing forms by ignoring the structure as a boundary or a barrier."[20] Unlike a skateboarder, unmediated by a board and wheels, a traceur's body comes into direct contact with his or her dance partner—the city itself. "The sport . . . doesn't leave marks on pavement, benches and rails, as skateboarding and in-line skating can, and there is no noise from ball bearings and hard landings."[21] And unlike skateboarders—who usually mine a particular site for its potential until they master it—traceurs *travel,* so by definition they do not loiter.

When traceurs theorize their own practice, they tend not to frame what they do in terms of a Marxist critique, as skaters like Stecyk tend to do. Traceurs are far more likely to address space qua space—"Freestyle Parkour, as you may have realised, is really all about space. Or, rather, the use of space. Whether you are slicing through it at pace, filling it with motion-art, sizing it up for the upcoming vault . . . it's all space"—and the obstacles within it that present the challenges that call on their skills: "Y'see, space—cool as it is with its whole omni-directional thing going on—has a nasty habit of filling up with shit which is just waiting to stub toes and trip people up. Shit loves doing that. Shit lives for that."[22] As David Thomson points out, "Parkour is not so much a manifesto as an instance of the unruly intersection between capital flow and the flow of human bodies; instead of coinciding, they may intersect at angles of varying and appositional intensities."[23]

Despite what traceurs say about their own practice, parkour is consistently represented and marketed as a useful set of skills for the urban outlaw, though it is difficult to say just what about parkour could be construed as illegal. If traceurs appear to run from the authorities, it is because the primary goal of parkour is to travel quickly and efficiently through space, to move on. And where Thomson writes of the traceur as wandering in a city, photographs, advertisements, sports marketing materials, and commercial films have linked parkour to a timeless, "already there," city, traceurs reinforcing singular symbols of urbanism and progress. This imaginary, static city is most frequently populated by strong young criminals, usually young men of color, whose travels through space resemble acts of fleeing from rather than moving toward. This sharp disconnection between the goal of parkour—to get somewhere beautifully—and its representation—to flee artfully—not only raises questions about the power of the representational apparatus to deform the art form, to rob it of its aura, so to speak, but also questions the nature of spectatorship itself. Parkour as a critique of capitalist space is implicit, but representations of the individual free-runs of traceurs in advertisements and movies reappropriate the critique. Parkour has been reconceived by the media—nearly beyond recognition—as a counterculture extreme sport in the spirit of skateboarding, whose practitioners (often members of an ethnic minority) compete to execute dangerous moves, practice in places charged with ideological significance, and engage in criminal activity. Parkour, as the media represents it, then, is an instance of a chain of signs referring to nothing but other signs, the "hyperreal" "bad boys" of parkour no longer involved in the reinvigoration of failed capitalist space but instead incorporated into a myth of an underworld network of criminals coaxed to the surface—running free but contained within the powerful city.

Parkour as Representation: Strong Young Criminals

Since the circulation of the *Jump London* series of parkour videos in 2003, sneaker companies have marketed free-running/parkour shoes to traceurs. Reebok in particular has racialized parkour—using nearly exclusively young men of color in their ad campaigns—while simultaneously linking parkour to illegal activities such as trespassing, vandalism, and graffiti tagging, in what seems to be a willful misunderstanding of the philosophy behind the sport. An early attempt at making a parkour shoe was Reebok's Wrapshear, one of several sneakers in the Barrio RBK line, which positioned the potential wearer as an urban outlaw who needed special shoes to help him outrun the police. All advertisements in the Barrio line featured African American or Latino models and spokespersons.[24] The Barrio RBK Web site features a young Latino man sitting on a skateboard in front of a graffiti-filled wall, wearing the "Barrio Wrapshear" parkour shoe, a can of spray paint by his side. When the user clicks the "custom fit dial" on the side of the shoe—a dial designed to look like a bottle cap—a new window opens, and a tangle of skyscrapers grows from the shoe, giving the viewer a bird's eye view of the city. We then follow the path of a man on the ground, who, in the next sequence, runs through the blighted city streets, scaling walls, jumping from rooftops, and vaulting a chain-link fence.[25]

Many readers will be familiar with the parkour scene in the 2006 remake of the James Bond film *Casino Royale.* Set in a war-torn country in Africa, Sebastien Foucan plays a bomb maker for in-country heroin dealers. Daniel Craig as Bond chases Foucan through an African village in order to find the drug lord's hideout—pursuing him through a landscape of half-completed, half-defunct building projects, ultimately finding the drug-dealers' lair. Other examples include David Belle's appearance as an underworld "neighborhood boss" in Luc Besson's *Banlieue 13,* or *B13,*[26] with an opening sequence showing Belle pursued from rooftop to rooftop by a group of gangbangers.[27] A New Line Cinema film, currently titled *Parkour,* slated for release in 2009, features Channing Tatum as "a renegade New York City cop who must infiltrate the underground world of free running, known as parkour, to bust a seemingly unstoppable gang of bank robbers."[28]

"Leave No Trace": The Pursuit of Flow

The media-constructed myth of parkour departs significantly from its practice, while retaining enough traces of its history to naturalize the myth as authentic. The discussion board for the 2009 *Parkour* on the Internet Movie Database is filled with traceur comments regarding this upcoming film, such as: "What kind of traceur or traceuse would rob a bank?" Another traceur responds: "It's fiction." It *is* fiction, of course, and this traceur's question is certainly similar to one a surfer might ask about *Point Break*—what kind of surfer would rob a bank?—or a mixed martial artist might ask of *Fight Club.* Bloggers and message posters on parkour Web sites like urbanfreeflow.com and americanparkour.com all voice a similar frustration with these films that depict traceurs as criminals, because they miss the mark of what parkour is "all about." If parkour is "all about space" and "flow" and community, they ask, why can't Hollywood get it right?

Among the things Hollywood doesn't get right in its representations of parkour is the insistence that it is practiced in cities, and this construction of parkour as an urban practice suggests a "natural" connection to crime.[29] According to one traceur, "Why can't they get a real traceur? Or why do they need to ruin the art by making a crappy b movie? And I bet they put an urban twist on it and that won't help out the already bad media about it. . . . A lot of people just think that what we do is just reckless tresp***ing."[30] Early newspaper coverage of parkour generated human interest pieces that also insisted on parkour's connection to the urban, a typical story depicting a crew of suburban kids taking a commuter train into the big city, leaping around Grand Central Station.[31] This urban connection spilled over into other representations until it became a "fact" of parkour. A survey of parkour sites and parkour videos on YouTube reveals that traceurs themselves know the difference between parkour as they practice it and parkour as the media shows it. This difference is not always perceived as negative, and films of exciting urban free-runs are greeted with enthusiasm, as long as the traceur is not a character whose free-running purpose is criminal or disrespectful of the environment.

It is impossible to say whether some traceurs are criminals, and others not, whether some traceurs trespass and vandalize. It does seem likely that in an activity that demands forward movement at all times, and that requires no equipment whatsoever, where cans of spray paint or other props of urban vandals would weigh a traceur down, that crime is antithetical to parkour, for strictly practical reasons. It is certainly possible to assert that the traceur's stated philosophy includes above all else personal safety, the safety of others, and respect for the environment. The "Leave No Trace" campaign sponsored by several parkour organizations is one example of the traceurs' efforts to connect with their communities. This worldwide campaign encourages parkour crews to spend time in the places they practice, cleaning up garbage, smoothing out rough edges on playground equipment, ensuring that their training areas are clean and safe—for their own practice, as well as for other users of these spaces.

Parkour and Its Audiences

In a 1992 *Performing Arts Journal* interview conducted soon after his publication of *The Audience,* Herbert Blau spoke of the first impulses of theatre, both the historical origin—or myth of origin—of theatrical representation and the conditions that must be met for a theatrical event to occur in the present, theatre's "materialization from whatever it is it was not."[32] The sudden appearance of the black-clad traceurs at the Forest Theatre illustrates what Blau means by the power of mere consciousness to call an audience into a condition of theatre: "Whatever we were doing before *this* moment was occurring without consciousness of a relationship that has now been theatricalized. The theatricalization occurs simply by looking, with that inflection of consciousness we now call 'the gaze.'"[33] Since the conference scholars were now familiar with the history and practice of parkour, since we had seen photographs of traceurs and had theorized the practice in terms of "outdoor performance," the question "Was that parkour?" pointed up the differences between the practice and its media representations. Until that moment, few of us had ever seen a live free-run, and the relationship formed between us and the free-run created an instance of theatre, perhaps "its most minimal sensation,"[34] as Blau has said.

Parkour engages another aspect of the barest conditions of theatre that Blau identifies. As one traceur says, "It is well to remember that anything unmoving in nature is already dead or dying. At its heart, parkour is about growth and about development. . . . In short, it is about movement." Calling to mind Blau's observation that theatre always presents us with death, the actor onstage literally dying in front our eyes, this piece of traceur philosophy presents parkour as an intervention on this fact of death that any human body within a live representation is bound to show us.[35] Whether we view parkour as a reinvigoration of dead spaces or a series of intersections of bodies and capital flow, what is always present in parkour *is* the body. When we pay attention to these bodies, when we see parkour in real time, its practice becomes a way to think about the dying things around it, and around us—people, things in "nature," buildings. As Antonin Artaud has said, despite the progress made as a culture in his modern age, "I do not believe we have managed to revitalize the world we live in."[36] Perhaps all outdoor performance makes us see the transitory nature of the structures we use to frame our lives unfolding before us, as it reinforces the power of the body to revitalize them. In pageantry this structure might be the piece of ground marked as sacred by a particular community, and an outdoor historical drama might hold the story itself as a marker of a shared history—the story revitalized each time it is played for an audience, remaining intact and "true," played as it is on the very site of its first impulse. Seen in this light, the traceur free-run that interrupted Scott Parker's oral history of the Forest Theatre was not merely an ironic contribution to the discussions we were having about the various types of "outdoor performance." Instead, it was an instance of theatre that called our attention to the structure at hand, a civic cultural space where dramas are performed, where people "play," and whose ongoing vitality depends on its engagement with the outdoors and with bodies, whether they are the bodies of stage actors or of a crew of running interlopers on their way from here to there.

Notes

1. Herbert Blau, "The Play of Thought: An Interview with Herbert Blau," *Performing Arts Journal* 14, no. 3 (1992): 1–32.

2. "Infilspeak Dictionary," Infiltration, www.infiltration.org/resources-infilspk.html (accessed May 22, 2008).

3. Female parkour practitioners are frequently called by the French feminine form *traceuses.*

4. David Belle, quoted at www.sfparkour.com (accessed Jan. 16, 2009).

5. "olleyt," "Travel Forum-Open Board," at Globosapiens, www.globosapiens.net, posted May 16, 2004 (accessed Feb. 8, 2009).

6. Hamish Malcolm, "Freestyle Parkour: Moving Beyond Boundaries," www.omissionofmercy.blogspot.com/2005/06/finally.html (accessed Feb. 8, 2009).

7. *The Tribe: Tutorial Volume 1,* DVD, dir. Mike Yamrus (Mark Toorock Management). The year of copyright is not noted in the DVD. This DVD, featuring a Washington, DC–based parkour crew called "The Tribe," is available through the American Parkour Web site, www.americanparkour.com (accessed Feb. 8, 2009).

8. Cynthia Jean Cohen Bull, "Looking at Movement as Culture: Contact Improvisation to Disco," in *Moving History/Dancing Cultures: A Dance History Reader,* ed. Ann Dils and Ann Cooper Albright (Middletown, CT: Wesleyan University Press, 2001), 406.

9. Infiltrators intentionally seek out forbidden places—particularly secured buildings and abandoned industrial sites—break into them, and then report their findings to fellow infiltrators through blogs and message boards.

10. Nigel Reynolds, "'Spiderman' trailer thrills viewers," *Daily Telegraph,* April 19, 2002.

11. The most popular "parkour song" is arguably Madonna's 2006 "Jump."

12. *Casino Royale,* DVD, dir. Martin Campbell (2006; Culver City: Sony Pictures Home Entertainment, 2007).

13. Michel de Certeau, *The Practice of Everyday Life,* trans. Steven Rendall (Berkeley: University of California Press, 2002), 49.

14. Henri Lefebvre, *The Production of Space,* trans. Donald Nicholson-Smith (Oxford: Blackwell, 1991), 167.

15. David Thomson, "Jump City: Parkour and the Traces," *South Atlantic Quarterly* 107, no. 2 (Spring 2008): 251–63.

16. Jane Jacobs, *The Death and Life of Great American Cities* (New York: Random House, 1961), 87.

17. Iain Borden, *Skateboarding, Space, and the City* (Oxford: Berg, 2001).

18. *Dogtown and Z-Boys,* DVD, dir. Stacy Peralta (2001; Culver City: Sony Pictures Classics, distributed by Columbia TriStar Home Entertainment, 2002).

19. *Urban Explorers: Into the Darkness,* DVD, dir. Melody Gilbert (2007; co-produced by Melody Gilbert and Channel Z Films).

20. "A Natural Perspective," www.urbanfreeflow.com/2008/12/26/a-natural-perspective/ (accessed Feb. 9, 2009).

21. Alex Dominguez, "Free form Exercise imported from France lets you stretch your imagination," *St. Louis Post-Dispatch,* Five Star Late Lift Edition, April 4, 2005, 6.

22. D. Edwardes, "Spatial Awareness or How to Avoid Shit," www.urbanfreeflow.com/2008/12/26/spatial-awareness/ (accessed Feb. 8, 2009).

23. Thomson, "Jump City," 251–52.

24. Reebok's skateboarding DGK ("Dirty Ghetto Kids") shoe campaign uses Stevie Williams as its spokesperson. Williams, called "the Allen Iverson of skateboarding," is shown in a movie feature on the Reebok Web site, sitting on a curb in his hometown of Philadelphia, eating a cheesesteak, his DGK skateboarding sneakers planted on the garbage-strewn street.

25. "BarrioRBK," http://showcase.latin3.com/reebok/barriorbk/default.html (accessed Feb. 8, 2009).

26. *Banlieue 13,* DVD, dir. Luc Besson (2004; Los Angeles: Magnolia Home Entertainment, 2006).

27. David Belle and Sebastien Foucan are rumored to have had a falling out regarding the use of parkour in their films, and Belle is regarded in the parkour community as having remained a purist. Foucan, who appears in *Casino Royale,* is the spokesperson for K-Swiss parkour athletic shoes.

28. Internet Movie Database, www.imdb.com/title/tt0968767/. This film does not yet have a title. *Parkour* is its working title.

29. It is also important to note that nearly all characters in movies with parkour depict male traceurs. Traceuses are conspicuously underrepresented in these films.

30. J-Boogs. "What the . . . ," Parkour General Discussion, www.spartafitness.com (accessed May 26, 2008).

31. Anna Bahney, "New Way for Teenagers to See If They Bounce," *New York Times,* March 28, 2004, late edition (East Coast), www.proquest.com.offcampus.lib.washington.edu (accessed April 3, 2004).

32. Blau, "The Play of Thought," 6.

33. Ibid.

34. Ibid.

35. Herbert Blau, "Spacing Out in the American Theater," in *The Dubious Spectacle: Extremities of Theater, 1976–2000* (Minneapolis: University of Minnesota Press, 2002), 51.

36. Antonin Artaud, "No More Masterpieces," in *The Theatre and Its Double,* trans. Mary Caroline Richards (New York: Grove Press, 1958), 83.

Symposium Response

Theatre Symposium attendees;
Jay Malarcher, moderator

[EDITOR'S NOTE: At several points in the discussion, the actual speaker became obscured to the point that the transcript cannot distinguish speakers. In cases where the speaker is known, such indication is made.]

JAY MALARCHER [JM]: Ideally this Symposium Response is a chance for the keynoters to chime in on some of the papers they've heard, some of the ideas that might have been suggested in the papers that add to their body of knowledge, add to something that they conceive of. What they did yesterday at the roundtable (since we were all there for it), you got the idea that they were speaking very specifically about their areas of interest. Now, let's just sort of open it up and respond to connections among papers; you know, within the panels most of the time they were fairly coherent, but there might be a paper from a panel on Friday that actually speaks more directly to a panel on Sunday, and again that's one of the beggaries of putting a conference together, not knowing from the abstract the full import of an idea.

AUDIENCE MEMBER [AM]: Something I found in all of the papers, taken as a group, was the way that sites can be shaped by a performance and then how it works the other way: it's a dialectical relationship. That's really exciting for me because my particular interest was the, the invigoration of a site that had no ideological or historical significance to anyone in any kind of shorthand way. Talking about a performance activity—that brings that site to life. It names it, you know, even just for a moment. And then others were talking about how important the actual site of something happened, that happened to a community that was historically significant, which could resonate not only with that performance but with the ideas of democracy and American history and, I think although not always expressly stated, constructions of race and ethnicity, especially in the American imagination. So that's something that really excited me about this topic was that in talking about inside and outside and the way that, that Susan [Kattwinkel] kind of started the whole conference, we're not talking about a one-way relationship, and that it, it just opened up my thinking, about how it can work both ways.

JM: The expression "site-specific" was mentioned more than anything else (except "outdoor historical drama"), and that's great: the relationship with the audience again. And for those of us who saw *Amadeus* last night, I can't conceive of PlayMakers having any kind of really deep-rooted idea about the relationship of the audience to that play, whereas most of the plays and performances we've been talking about very much included the audience in the dialogue. The actor-audience relationship is palpable in these plays. And in something like Austin's thing, *Esther's Follies,* that's knowing who's around, you know; it's almost like, if history includes today, then that's an historical drama as well because that's who we are in Austin and this . . . it's almost like *Our Town*. [laughter] . . . I'm going into the stage manager speech: "This is who we are in Austin, Texas, on this Friday night." It's kind of a weird way of looking at it, but again, it maybe shows the democratization of the drama in these, in these kinds of forms.

AM: Well, there's something about moving outside that automatically does that because outside is more site-specific than inside. Inside, you could be in any building in any place that happens to be built that way, but as soon as you're outside, you're in a very specific place. Besides that, that ends up being an element of any performance that's outdoors, because it's outdoors and therefore the specific place of it becomes very important, just like as I mentioned yesterday, I think the other thing that happens as soon as you move outdoors is you lose an element of control, which is another interesting thing you have, and the spectators automatically become a part of it. So what this weekend has made very clear to me is that any time you have any element of a performance outside, it automatically becomes something very different than a performance that happens inside. It just has its own set of issues and problems.

JM: Another word that came up over and over again was *authenticity,* and the idea that when you go inside of a theatre building, an institutional theatre, you understand that everything is sort of controlled and designed, whereas when you go outside, the moon might be taken into account, but it's not designed—it's present to everyone in a very real way. Whether it's the site-specific authenticity that we've discussed, or the authenticity of the weather that's affecting everyone at the moment, it's a nice variable to bring in.

Mark R. Sumner [MRS]: I thought that the different presentations, some, almost the presentation of vaudeville type material, others the presentation of pageant material, some outdoor drama, would have brought us to the point where you just almost did, and I think you're thinking that way, that the location, as I think Scott pointed out—very clearly—the location is part of the performance, and the moment when you think about staging anything outdoors, you must think of the audience from the time they look for your amphitheatre, until they park, until they have gotten to a seat, and then you also have to present them [with] something worthwhile, which obviously we all try to do. But the performance starts with a location. You have to find it, and you have to find a way back from it: all of which you may have to lean on the state to get done, which brings up something that I don't think was mentioned much by anybody except the federal theatre paper, and I'm sorry I had to miss a couple, and so it may have been covered but that thought is that, if you're going to build a kind of community entrance and community support, you have got to pay attention to politics in your community, in your state. It is important that you know the people at some point or someone who knows them, so that if you need to talk to them about highway signs, you know where to go and what to do.

Now, if you're the director, this is not your problem. If you're an actor, this is not your problem. If you're the playwright, it's not your problem. But if you're the manager, or the producer, or the scenic designer or any one of a number of other things, you must think of the politics. Of course, the wise thing to remember is that your company is not political, at least in local terms, that you are for everybody who's doing a good job . . . no matter what flavor they may be or where they come from. If they're doing a good job, you folks are all for 'em, especially if they're helping you, but you sometimes have to beg, sometimes you have to borrow, but I won't use the other word. [laughter] Thank you.

Scott J. Parker [SJP]: Jay, when I first heard about the subject for the seminar, I was thrilled by the idea; and, I, in my typical myopic way of thinking about outdoor drama, I thought this was gonna be all about outdoor historical drama. Well, this has been a tremendous eye-opener for me, to learn about so many different ways of producing outdoors that I knew a little bit about the inner drama, but not as much as I learned today in the parkour and the project in Austin. The railroad projects, I knew nothing about; I learned more about the Mormon pageants than I knew before. It really has pointed out how narrow my focus had become, and you've opened it up considerably, and I want to thank you all for learning all about this.

JM: Absolutely! That's one of the benefits of this whole exercise, but if you remember the call for papers, I invited papers on Greek drama and, and Shakespearean, historical, you know, in his own time. I didn't get a lot of papers on those; in fact, as you see, you know, nobody really touched on those enough, but they did, some people did reference them, right? Going back to the ritual of the hillside theatre and, and the roots of what we might call Western drama.

AM: *Agamemnon.*

JM: *Agamemnon,* right, yeah. Alive and well. Or maybe not so well. But, no, the idea that, that, theatre is widening its topics as well, I mean, theatre in general—to performance studies and whatnot—it's fun that we do expand the idea of outdoor drama as not being in the hands of one group but as open and available. If you've got the right product, if you've got the right message or story to tell, it's a really viable, still viable, maybe not in the sense of, you know, opening up a, you know, twenty-five-million-dollar complex and running for a hundred years, but it's viable enough if you know, if you know your scope, and again, I didn't know about airdomes, I thought Zeppelins landed in them or something [laughter], which, hey, you know, maybe, sometime somebody did do a balloon act or whatever. Anyway . . .

MRS: I would like to remind everybody, Jay, that the Institute of Outdoor Drama has a bibliography that presents articles and books by the people who built the outdoor historical drama and the Shakespeare festivals, and a lot of that is available. Because, if you're going outdoors, one thing is a fact: that technical work is there; and how it's been done somewhere else will often explain to you how to proceed just from reading some of the material and also give you plenty of ammunition as to why to proceed . . . and of course, you have to watch out for playwrights like me. [laughter]

I wrote a play—and I told you about it—and it won a contest at a very young time because I had been in the Boy Scouts, and I had studied the

Indians, and I admired them, and I felt that their ability to deal with the world around them was superlative and that everybody ought to learn something about it. And so, I wrote a play, basing it on the fact that the Cherokee Indians were just next door to where I grew up. The only thing is I'd not been a Cherokee.

I found out after the play won a prize, after it was produced in the Playmaker theatre here, that I had written a play about the Plains Indians, not about the Cherokee as I had said, which taught me to read a little more the next time I had a chance to write something (and I don't tell that part of the story very often, but I thought John Harris would get a smile out of it).

JM: Nice. Yes?

AM2: I just, realized, you know, that we were all talking about site-specific things, and I didn't get to show the last clip of the paper hand-puppet show, which was *The Librarian at Basra,* and I was thinking about that John Henry is an outdoor, you know, atmosphere and the village was certainly outdoors and the trees all came in and the Buddha was outdoors. [As for] *The Librarian at Basra,* what they do is they framed it, so it is a shadow-puppet in the white. But then you're not looking at the trees, you're looking, you know, in, in—

JM: It forces you indoors almost, yeah.

AM2: Yeah. So, it puts you indoors with the desert, and it's just basically a white very small frame, like maybe a eight-by-six-foot box with a black proscenium around it and then the white and the black, so you have to, you know, gear in; you have to focus in to see it, and then you don't see all the outside trees and the things that remind you where you're at.

AM3: I think this is one other thing of confession time is that when in doing *Josiah* and producing it, I was so into the trenches about trying to get the show done, that there was a Native American costume because when Josiah was escaping, he ran into a group, and Rusty had written it into the script, couldn't afford the costume, so I cut the scene, which would have been fine if I had talked to Rusty, and I didn't. And then, the gentleman who had been hired to compose the music is the late Frank Lewin. Frank died earlier this year, but listening to the music myself, I didn't think it quite merged with African American experience or expectation of African American experience. And so I changed it, which would have been cool if I had talked to Frank. So, it was like a dress rehearsal, the builder who had built the house was a builder, and he built a house instead of a prop in which case it was like making grooves into the floor of this new thing, but I was like going crazy 'cause people were coming the next day, and Frank and Rusty were there, and they sat there, and they watched the whole show and, after it was over, went off into a corner; and they were looking at me, and Rusty did say something to the effect of, "I could tear you a new butthole; don't ever do that again. I know you, [and] I know that there wasn't malice of forethought, but people get sued over that. Don't do that anymore, but congratulations that the show is up." Frank was a little more pissed and said, "I don't want to, I don't like how this happened; I don't like the way that I've been treated. I don't want to stop the show, but my name can't go on this." And so the program was at the press that night, and [I] had to call over [and instruct the printer to] take his name out. So, if you look in the program, you know, "written by Rusty Mundell," duh-da, duh-da, da, there's a big hole in the program—and that's where we took Frank's name out. And to be as upset as he should have been and without discussion . . . he was very gracious about it, but, it's like, I have felt bad about that to this day, and now he's died and I can't say anything to him, you know, that it happened twenty years ago. As an element of outdoor drama, because I think that was something else, I don't think any of the papers directly addressed was sound: music, voices, particularly in outdoor spaces.

AM4: And I'd like to point out about Frank, too, because Frank composed the music for *Beyond the Sundown,* and just so people know of the quality that was happening in some of the music that was composed for these productions, Frank was nominated for a Pulitzer Prize in music for his composition work.

AM5: He wrote the *Requiem* for Kennedy's assassination.

AM6: He was a Yale professor.

AM7: Yeah, and he, you know, I mean, just first-class wonderful music of a very high caliber. So . . .

JM: And you know actually that, that comment and that description points to something else we may not have touched on enough, and that is how unified these pieces had to be, you know, in the presentation of the spectacle, the text, the music, the whole experience as we've talked about you know, the story is not just one of those elements; the story is how everything plays together, so that's a really interesting thing; if any of you are enhancing your papers, that might be a way to go a little deeper, if that's something that you can research, namely the interaction—the collaboration—that goes into mounting something huge like this.

JANE BARNETTE [JB]: With the railroad pageant—the original *Railroads on Parade*—when it was in New York had music by Kurt Weill, and one of the things that I have the hardest trouble with was figuring out what they did with the music when it went to Chicago, because it was very much stolen from Weill. So in my case, I would say, without having heard the music, but knowing Weill's work, I would imagine it was quite good, but it's just one of those mysteries of still trying to put the pieces together in terms of what they actually did.

JM: Right, maybe they used some of the *Happy End* music since it said "Chicago."

Well, I hear a lull. I thank you again! Safe travels back to wherever you came from, and we'll see you at another Theatre Symposium, I hope, finding a topic that is near and dear to you.

This one, again, the first thing I told you is that I'm not really big on, or not up on, outdoor drama as a whole, and I learned, as I think if I speak for everyone, you know, please apologize if I'm overstepping, you know, this is eye-opening as Scott said and broadens our horizon, so thanks again for . . . yes, Mark?

MRS: Just to add a final quote from Paul Green that I meant to say yesterday but forgot and that is that, in talking about *The Lost Colony,* and the play that he was then writing called *A Common Glory,* that Paul said, "I want to write not what is; I want to make people understand what should be." And I think most of the people that have followed his path in writing have felt the same way.

JM: Thank you so much.

Contributors

Keynote Speakers

Rob Franklin Fox is the director for the Institute of Outdoor Drama at the University of North Carolina at Chapel Hill. He served as general manager for PlayMakers Repertory Company from 1999 to 2007. Fox had been with the Department of Dramatic Art in the College of Arts and Sciences at UNC Chapel Hill for more than ten years. He has served as a lecturer, teaching a course in theatre management. Fox began his stay at UNC Chapel Hill as an assistant box office manager for PlayMakers Repertory Company in 1997.

Fox has fourteen years of theatre management experience and holds a Master of Business Administration degree in Arts Management from Oklahoma City University. While at OCU he performed with the OCU Children's Theatre and was box office manager for Oklahoma Opera and Musical Theater Company. He has served as box office manager for the American Dance Festival in Durham, North Carolina, and Florida Studio Theatre in Sarasota, Florida. Fox earned his BA in history from Belhaven College in Jackson, Mississippi. While at Belhaven, he performed with The Socks and Buckskins Players and The Millsaps Players. He is past president of the Triangle Network of Theaters, former board member of the Canton Community Players, and a member of the North Carolina Theatre Conference.

Scott J. Parker was, from 1990 until his retirement in 2007, the director of the Institute of Outdoor Drama, a national advisory and research agency at the University of North Carolina at Chapel Hill, which serves

110 outdoor theatres in thirty-seven states (historical dramas, Shakespeare festivals, religious dramas) and thirty communities across the country, developing new outdoor theatres. During his seventeen years at the IOD he conducted forty feasibility studies in twenty-five states, planned and presided over seventeen national conferences, and advised more than one hundred organizations across the country on the development of new nonprofit theatre companies.

He is the former producer of Paul Green's *The Lost Colony,* the nation's first outdoor historical drama located on Roanoke Island, North Carolina, and coauthor of *Creating Historical Drama* (2005), a resource book for playwrights and professional and amateur theatres.

He taught in the Drama Department at Duke University as its managing director for six years, was a professor and managing director for seven years in the Theatre Department at East Carolina University, and in the late 1970s managed entertainers for Walt Disney World in Orlando. Scott holds an MFA in directing from the University of Virginia, an MA in Dramatic Art from the University of North Carolina at Chapel Hill, and a BA in English from Guilford College, which presented him with its Alumni Excellence Award in 2002.

On graduation from college in 1968, Scott entered the U.S. Army, where he served as a television production specialist for two years at the White House, the Pentagon, and Fort Belvoir, Virginia.

He is a former president of the National Theatre Conference based in New York City, is a founding member of the Association for Theatre in Higher Education, and has traveled throughout the country as an adjudicator for the American College Theatre Festival and the Festival of American Community Theatre. He was a chief regional officer for the American Theatre Association and has served as president of the Southeastern Theatre Conference, the North Carolina Theatre Conference (which presented him with the Marian A. Smith Distinguished Career Award in 2007), the North Carolina Association of Professional Theatres, and Arts Advocates of North Carolina, a professional lobbying organization. Since 1990 he has been the vice president of the Paul Green Foundation.

In 2000 he was inducted into the College of Fellows of the American Theatre, the honor society based at the John F. Kennedy Center for the Performing Arts in Washington, DC, and is currently serving as dean of the college. In 1992 he received the Suzanne M. Davis Award for distinguished service to theatre in the South by the Southeastern Theatre Conference, and in 1991 he was elected to membership of the Players Club in New York City. In 2007 he was elected as only the third Lifetime Member of the Shakespeare Theatre Association of America.

Mark R. Sumner grew up with ready access to the newsrooms of the *Asheville Citizen,* where his father was a journalist. His first paid job was as a string correspondent for that newspaper, reporting school news at age fourteen.

He wrote his first play while a high school student in Asheville, North Carolina, during the fall of 1938. It won a state playwriting prize. *The Scarlet Arrow* was produced for presentation at the statewide drama festival at Playmakers Theatre at the University of North Carolina at Chapel Hill, launching Sumner on a career in theatre work. He had two short prizewinning contest plays, *Rock Dust* and *Thunderhead,* published when he came back from serving in the army during World War II.

He spent time as an actor, as a stage director, and as a theatre manager after getting two degrees from the University of North Carolina at Chapel Hill and serving as publicity director for the famed Carolina Playmakers.

In recent years he has written not only *Pathway to Freedom* for Snow Camp, North Carolina, but *Dreams and Drill Bits* and *Black River Traders* for Farmington, New Mexico.

Sumner, who also wrote *Young Washington* for Pennsylvania, was director of the Institute of Outdoor Drama at the University of North Carolina at Chapel Hill for twenty-five years. During that time he served as producer of Paul Green's *The Lost Colony,* was president of the ten-state Southeastern Theatre Conference, and served on the boards of the United States Institute of Theatre Technology and the American Theatre Association. As director of the IOD he helped start thirty outdoor theatre companies in twenty-six states.

He is a member of the Paul Green Foundation Board of Trustees, Actors' Equity Association, the Society of Stage Directors and Choreographers, and the Dramatists Guild. He is also a member of the College of Fellows of the American Theatre at the John F. Kennedy Center for the Performing Arts and a member of the National Theatre Conference.

Sumner is married to the former Glenn Geddings, of Cranford, New Jersey, and has six children and nine grandchildren.

Authors

Jane Barnette is the resident dramaturg and theatre historian in the Department of Theatre and Performance Studies at Kennesaw State University. She has published articles in *Theatre Symposium* and *Theatre InSight,* reviews in *Theatre Journal,* and has presented at national and international conferences regularly since 1995. Her research interests include train culture, gender and American studies, pageantry and alterity, and the pedagogy of theatre history/theory.

Charlotte Headrick is a professor of theatre arts, coordinator of the University Theatre, and associate chair of the Department of Speech Communication at Oregon State University. She holds a PhD in drama from the University of Georgia. She is the 1994 Elizabeth P. Ritchie Outstanding Professor for Undergraduate Teaching, the highest teaching award of Oregon State University, and she received the 2003 Excellence Award from the College of Liberal Arts, the highest honor given by the college. She has directed the American premieres of several Irish plays, including *Signora Joyce,* by Gemma O'Connor; *Love and a Bottle,* by Declan Hughes; *Treehouses,* by Elizabeth Kuti; *Heritage,* by Nicola McCartney; and *Lay Up Your Ends,* by Charabanc Theatre Company. Additionally, she has directed *Eclipsed,* by Patricia Burke Brogan; *Tea in a China Cup,* by Christina Reid; and *Twinkletoes,* by Jennifer Johnston. Her articles and reviews on Irish theatre have appeared in *Nua, Theatre Symposium, Northwest Theatre Review, Working Papers in Irish Studies, Irish Literary Supplement, Hungarian Journal of English and American Studies,* and *The Encyclopedia of Ireland.* Other essays have appeared in *Theatre Journal, Southern Theatre, Contemporary Theatre Review, Comparative Literature and Culture,* and *Hypermedia Joyce Studies.* She has presented numerous papers on Irish theatre nationally and internationally, particularly on the work of Irish women dramatists. She is the recipient of the Kennedy Center Medallion for outstanding service to the Kennedy Center/American College Theatre Festival and of the Hovland Service Award for Oregon State. She is the past editor of the online journal *Siar* (Western Institute for Irish Studies). She is coeditor, along with Eileen Kearney, of a volume of Irish plays by women *(Women of Ireland)* to be published by Syracuse University Press. She is a member of Actors Equity Association.

Jeanmarie Higgins is a PhD candidate in theatre history and criticism at the University of Washington. Her current research concerns the production of urban space through theatrical and paratheatrical performance. She holds an MFA in playwriting from the University of Virginia and teaches critical theory at Cornish College of the Arts. This is her first published article.

Martha S. LoMonaco is professor of theatre and resident theatre director for the Department of Visual and Performing Arts at Fairfield University. She is a widely published theatre historian and lecturer and serves as president of the Theatre Library Association, an international scholarly organization dedicated to the documentation and preservation of performing arts collections. Her most recent book, *Summer Stock! An American Theatrical Phenomenon,* was named a *Choice* Outstanding Academic Title of 2004. She is currently researching a book on American history as tourist performance, which will consider how history and popular mythology are disseminated, celebrated, and commodified through theatrical presentations. Dr. LoMonaco was elected in 2007 to the League of Professional Theatre Women based in New York City.

Landis K. Magnuson is the former chair of the English department and continues to serve as director of the Anselmian Abbey Players at Saint Anselm College in Manchester, New Hampshire. His book *Circle Stock Theater: Touring American Small Towns, 1900–1960* was designated by *Choice* as an Outstanding Academic Book. His scholarship has centered on American theatre of the late nineteenth century and early twentieth, including such popular forms as repertoire theatre, vaudeville, the Chautauqua movement, and Swedish-dialect plays. His recent research has appeared in *Theatre History Studies* and *Theatre Design and Technology.*

Angela Sweigart-Gallagher is a freelance teaching artist and grant writer in New York City. She recently completed her PhD in Theatre and Drama at the University of Wisconsin, Madison. Her current research focuses on the representation of "America" within the productions of the Federal Theatre Project. This is her first published article.

Andrew Vorder Bruegge serves as chair of the Department of Theatre and Dance at Winthrop University, where he teaches theatre history and literature, as well as early dance, and directs and choreographs departmental productions. He is active in a number of professional organizations. He reviews books regularly for the Sixteenth Century Studies Conference; serves as a regional respondent for the American College Theatre Festival; serves on the steering committee of the ABC Project; and has reviewed textbooks for several major publishers. His past administrative experience includes artistic direction and/or management of several summer theatres and madrigal dinners; five years as the director of theatre at Bellarmine College; four years as chair of the Department of Theatre, Film Studies, and Dance at St. Cloud State University; and president of the Kentucky Theatre Association.

He has worked as a translator/adapter, director, performer, choreographer, and playwright. His directing credits include Sophocles' *Electra*, Arnold Wesker's *Roots*, Jean Racine's *Andromache*, John Webster's *The Duchess of Malfi*, and Tom Stoppard's *Travesties*. He has directed or choreographed productions of *Oklahoma!*, *The Mikado*, *Anything Goes*, *The Pirates of Penzance*, *Venus and Adonis*, *Godspell*, *Amahl and the Night Visitors*, and *The Fantasticks*. He has choreographed stage combat for productions of *Macbeth*, *Romeo and Juliet*, and *Cyrano de Bergerac*. He has translated various comedies by Alfred de Musset, as well as Jean Racine's *Phaedra* and *The Litigators* (including a special adaptation for the Kentucky Shakespeare Festival). In recent years Dr. Vorder Bruegge has turned his attention to playwriting. He has composed three full-length dramas: *The Transfiguration of Wonder Woman*, *The Widows of Ashur*, and *Alceste's Return*, a "sequel" to Molière's *The Misanthrope* that was given a staged reading at the Playwrights' Center in early 2005. Dr. Vorder Bruegge was the cofounder and codirector for more than a decade of the Roc Havre Dance Ensemble. During that time he led ensembles on tours to the United Kingdom, Mexico, and the Stratford (Ontario) Shakespeare Festival.

www.ingramcontent.com/pod-product-compliance
Lightning Source LLC
LaVergne TN
LVHW050604110926
847619LV00018B/150

* 9 7 8 0 8 1 7 3 5 5 5 5 5 *